PRAISE FOR
VISION BLOCKERS

"*Vision Blockers* is a must-have resource for entrepreneurs and leaders alike. Eric Scroggins shares secrets for successfully navigating life's challenges, while maintaining focus and vision toward one's destiny. Perfect for anyone in transition to a better self, *Vision Blockers* inspires a new approach for pursuing possibility."

— **Heather Allen MGIM-MBA, Author of**
Let Your Creativity Work for You

"This book will propel you from where you are to where you want to go! Apply this wisdom to your life and you will more clearly see your own vision and accomplish everything you desire!"

— **Patrick Snow, International Best-Selling Author of**
Creating Your Own Destiny* and *The Affluent Entrepreneur

"You can expect nothing less but to be recharged, focused, and fueled by Eric's book. If you finally want to realize your purpose, start here."

— **Michael Fulmore, Author of** *Unleashing Your Ambition*

"If you are looking for a powerful resource to help you break through barriers that are holding you back in life or at work, I highly recommend Eric Scroggins' book, *Vision Blockers*. As a Leadership and Teambuilding Coach, I work with people every day who are stuck—personally and professionally—and have a hard time seeing the opportunities that lie before them. This book is powerful because it taps into the soul of each of us and allows us to find the courage to focus on what's *right* about us, what's possible, and to stop focusing on the 'Vision Blockers' and self-destructing stories that hold us back."

— **Theresa Callahan, Author of** *Managing For Performance:*
Building Accountability for Team Success

"Have you ever felt that pull toward something greater, a pull that comes from a place rooted so deep you know in your heart it is your true direction, yet it is rooted so deep that the way there, the way from where you are now to where you want to be, is obscure and seemingly nonexistent? Through Eric Scroggins' book, through his lessons, and through his passion, you will find your way; you will find your way to the life you only thought could exist in a dream. Get ready to find your vision and live it."

— **Jennifer Lee Tracy, Author of**
Sincerely, The Mentor: A Journey of Perception

"I believe Eric has hit the mark dead center. Not only is his insight valuable, but it will help anyone move forward to power through any barrier. This book is for those of us with a dream!"

— **Jerome Midgette, Author, Teacher**

"Take heart, dear reader! You have an ally for change in Dr. Eric Scroggins! Eric understands what it is to be 'stuck' in life by visible and invisible ties that keep you blocked from fulfilling the amazing destiny you were created to experience! *Vision Blockers* will not only help you *identify and overcome* your blind spots but also help you find and fulfill the vision of your heart and begin to live the life of your dreams!"

— **Dana E. Morrison, Entrepreneur, Speaker, and Author of**
Transforming Your Life Now!

"Eric Scroggins has written a book that is a must read for every business person. He masterfully guides the reader to identifying his or her passion and beautifully helps you to discover the barriers to getting there. This is a book I will refer to many times."

— **Sheila Paxton, Author,** *Getting Past Jaded,* **Founder, Fit4Love**

"Vision Blockers is a blueprint for self-discovery. With gentle guidance, the author helps you break through barriers that stand in the way of applying your gifts, talents, needs, wants, and true desires, to uncover the real you—and the life you are destined to live."

— **Susan Friedmann, International Bestselling Author of** *Riches in Niches: How to Make it BIG in a small Market*

"Vision Blockers provides a unique fusion of timeless spiritual wisdom with the science of modern business to provide a powerful tool for success."

— **Jack L. Harris, Hands of Hope Foundation International (Iraq)**

"As a business owner, father of two (independently minded teens), and someone passionate about having mentors, I cannot recommend *Vision Blockers* enough. Eric has done an excellent job of providing a practical guide to realizing the importance of crafting your vision and integrating it into your life's journey. Whether it's change management, dealing with adversity, or merely getting 'unstuck,' his words ring true and clear and will lead you in building the framework to move through life in a meaningful and purposeful way."

— **Randall Broad, Author of** *It's an Extraordinary Life—Don't Miss It*

"In his dynamic new book, *Vision Blockers*, Eric Scroggins gives a clear blueprint to move your life forward and achieve your dreams. From his broad background and recognized achievements, Eric helps us understand the power of what Vision can do and how to navigate successfully through the vision process. His book gives us important insight to help us identify and overcome any 'Vision Blockers' that we may be facing. I heartily recommend this book for people who want their lives to move forward!"

— **Dr. Michael Maiden, Senior Pastor, Church for the Nations, Phoenix, Arizona**

"Motivational, inspirational, and full of great techniques for shattering barriers standing in your way, Eric Scroggins' *Vision Blockers* gives the reader a step-by-step process for removing obstacles permanently."

— **Lee Davis, Author of *Soaring From Within***

"Eric Scroggins' *Vision Blockers* takes the reader on a journey of discovery, learning about what stands in the way of your destiny and how to remove it. This is a must-read for anyone wanting more!"

— **Brett Dupree, Author of *Joyous Expansion***

"Whether you are a leader of a large company or a small business owner with a few employees, the concepts portrayed in *Vision Blockers* will help you take your company and your life to the next level."

— **Kathy Nelson, Owner Resonance Fitness Consulting**

"The tools and insights Eric Scroggins shares in his book have been instrumental in elevating my leadership and results. Anyone looking to strengthen his or her leadership skills and remove barriers should get to know the concepts shared here."

— **Charmaine Lee, Author, Speaker, Coach, Entrepreneur**

A LEADERSHIP ROAD MAP FOR EMBRACING CHANGE

VISION BLOCKERS

How to Shatter Barriers to
Achieve Your Destiny

Eric J. Scroggins, Ph.D.

DEDICATION

To the one I cherish the most, my beautiful wife Saundra. Thank you for being the best partner a man could ever have. We married on August 20, 1993 and are more madly in love now than on that day. Thank you for being my greatest fan and biggest support. I love you so much!

To my children, Dylan and Alyssa: You two have shown me the value of a father's love and taught me always to focus on the important thing—family. I pray you will always shatter the barriers to your destiny. I love you both!

ACKNOWLEDGMENTS

There are so many people to thank in a project like this. Every step in my journey through life I have been blessed by meeting some of the most incredible people. Each one has made a mark on me and helped me to become a better person. I have been enriched by you all.

I would especially like to recognize and thank the following people for their support, encouragement, and belief in my dreams:

My mother Mary Lou—Mom, you are the greatest, and I am so thankful for everything you have taught me along the way; your care and compassion during my roughest moments lives in me today.

My brother and two sisters—Erin, Stacey, and Melissa—thank you for making growing up a blast and giving me great memories.

Gary and Pat Ferguson—Thank you for investing your heart in a driven, passionate, and a bit over-the-top kid. Aside from giving me your daughter's hand, you have given me love and support.

Tony Bosmans—Thanks for the walks and the long talks growing up. Thanks for fanning the flame.

Mike Stone—My oldest and dearest friend. Thanks for everything!

Maurice Searles—Thank you for faithfully fighting every fight beside me! Our battles have been many and there aren't many soldiers like you.

All my Pastor Friends—Your prayers, your friendship, and your inspiration help me continue to go the distance and reach for the stars.

The Word of Life Church, Renton, WA—Thank you for allowing me to speak this message for the very first time.

The book team—Patrick Snow, Jamie McCormack, Tyler Tichelaar, Susan Friedmann, Shiloh Schroeder, Theresa Callahan, and all those who helped me move it forward—Thank you.

To you, the reader, for taking the first step in overcoming your Vision Blockers and making your dream a reality. God Bless!

CONTENTS

INTRODUCTION

Moving Forward

"It doesn't matter where you are coming from.
All that matters is where you are going."
— Brian Tracy

Throughout the years, countless individuals have simply been stuck! Stuck in a job that is going nowhere, stuck in a business that is not growing or giving the kind of return expected, stuck in a ministry that is having minimal impact, or stuck in a life that just doesn't seem to move forward. In each of these cases, the problem boils down to no vision, and without vision, there is no hope. One of the classic strategies of an enemy opponent is to block your vision and keep you from seeing the life you were supposed to live. I have written this book to address that very topic. Moving forward is all about overcoming your *vision blockers*—about getting you to see the life you were meant to live, the business you were meant to run, or the ministry you were meant to lead.

Whether you are leading a non-profit, for profit, church, organization, department, or division, the truth is "without vision the people perish." This old proverb makes clear that if there is no vision, people will revolt, dissipate, or become disconnected. That is probably right where you are—disconnected from your future, about to revolt if something doesn't change, or fading away into a dissipated life full of regrets. My goal is not to allow that to happen to you, but to put you on a course toward seeing exactly what you want, where you want to go, and how you are going to get there.

Let's start with a few questions that can set the foundation for this journey we will take together. Your answers to these questions will create the framework we will work from to overcome your vision blockers. They form the basis for a personal quest to learn more about yourself and more about what is getting in your way and keeping you from the life you know you were meant to live. Taking action on your responses will help you push past whatever barriers dare to stand in your way and propel you to a life of freedom, happiness, and prosperity.

Are you frustrated with your current job? Do you find yourself thinking about doing other things, but you don't know how? Are you unhappy with the impact you are currently having in your life? Does something bigger seem like it lives in you, but it can't escape? When you look at the world, are you moved by reports you hear of the living conditions some are forced to live with? Is your department, division, business, or ministry/organization not reaching the level you thought it should or making the impact you know it could? Do you sense your heart *calling* out for a change? Are you *really* happy? Are you truly doing what your heart is passionate about in both your personal and professional life?

As I speak around the world and meet thousands of people in various countries, I find that many people are not doing what they are passionate about. They are stuck in frustrating, overwhelming situations, and yet they have something inside of them calling out for something more. The reason they're stuck is that they have no vision. They absolutely can't see from point A to point B in their lives, and point B is where their destiny lies. Something is getting in the way and keeping them from seeing clearly the future or destiny they were meant to live. These same people are amazingly gifted, full of talents and skills that can make a global, world-changing impact, yet they are stuck doing mundane jobs with mediocre results. The amount of untapped capacity in people is overwhelming. I believe that a substantial number of the social issues we face, the financial crises that lurk, and the poverty experienced in the world can be overcome by good people taking action and executing on their visions. You really can live the life that seems just outside your reach—the life that your heart knows you are supposed to be living. But you must be willing to take the action necessary to push through the barriers and overcome the vision blockers to identify your destiny clearly. Are you willing?

Before you answer that, let me tell you that I have been in the same situation, having to work through my own vision blockers that would dare to keep me from my dreams. I spent years wandering around a vision, wallowing in my life's disappointments, and having my vision blocked by various circumstances, emotional wounds, and a series of letdowns. But through a process of pushing through and powering beyond each barrier set before me, I was able to launch into my life's passion. In this book, I will tell you more about how I did it, sharing that process so you can do the same.

Vision is defined as "the act or power of anticipating that which will or may come to be" and "an experience in which an event appears vividly or credibly to the mind, although not actually present but expected to be." Having vision is the ability to see what is to come so vividly, so clearly that it becomes a magnetic force drawing you to it. That is what's missing. To be something different, you have to see something different. Nothing in your life changes without first seeing that change is necessary and then developing a vision that includes that change. You must develop a "this situation must change" attitude. Clearly and concretely, holding that vision in your heart will compel your mind and your body to begin moving in that direction. Vision is the solution to a life standing still.

Throughout our lives, we encounter various obstacles, pick up habits, hold on to pain, fail to see things from a higher vantage point, or simply get so discouraged that we stop trying. Often, these things cause us simply to settle. Each one attaches to our lives and our hearts and begins to build walls or barriers that help keep us protected and shrouded. The barriers serve as protectors that prevent any further pain from developing or any further disappointment from happening. We live our lives behind these walls, and eventually, we have all the excuses we need so we never accomplish the kind of life we've always wanted to live. Each barrier builds on the last, each layer forms atop the next, and we create this very safe enclosure that serves one purpose and one purpose alone, keeping us from seeing ourselves as successful, powerful, and in charge of our future. Vision Blockers!

By the end of this book, I believe you will be able to identify your vision blockers, properly overcome each one, find the vision of your heart, and begin to live your life in that direction. Each chapter will take you on a journey to learn how each vision blocker works and to develop a strategy for overcoming it permanently. We will start at the beginning by learning the power of vision. In Chapter 1, you will see that each one of us is meant to have vision and that vision is conditionally based on a pure heart. Simply put, a pure heart is one without contamination, corruption, obstacle, or barrier. Gaining a clear understanding of the powerful effect vision can have on your life will inspire you to want one of your very own.

It will give you fuel to move through the next eight chapters, identifying each vision blocker that you anxiously await the secret to overcome. In these chapters, you will be challenged to look at your habits, decisions, and choices in life to determine whether they line up with your heart's calling. Brian Tracy said, "Successful people are simply those with successful habits." I trust you're reading this book because you want to be more successful, but that requires asking: What choices have you made in life that have led you to the life you currently lead? How do you face those decisions and redirect them into more productive, healthier habits and decisions that move you from where you are to where you want to be? Here you will learn the ABCs of correcting your aim and making better decisions that will begin to form a solid foundation upon which to build your vision.

You will also learn about the evil beneath the surface that is sabotaging each and every relationship, your social interactions, the way you think about others, and the effects this evil has on your vision. Wherever parents are fighting with kids, kids fighting with parents, spouses bickering, and coworkers at odds with one another, there is strife. This culprit is birthed out of insecurity and lives in bitterness, becoming a consuming force that keeps your vision at bay. You will learn how to move beyond this chaos causer and into a realm of peace, which is the atmosphere your vision needs to take on its form, function, and life.

Fear is a paralyzing force in many lives. Regardless of whether you are afraid of heights, afraid of public speaking, or afraid of taking on any new challenges, fear grips your heart and mind, paralyzing you from making decisions or taking action to live out your dream. The truth is that fear is nothing more than False Evidence Appearing Real. The games the mind plays, the trigger of your emotional system designed to keep you safe, can move you beyond the safety mechanism to the place where you won't move at all. To help you overcome this paralysis, I will share my experience in Cheju Do Island and the wisdom I learned from the great drill instructors there who teach the art of rappelling. Gaining a "Just Jump" perspective will help you "repel" your fear to move to a place of power.

In these pages, you will find inspiration to embrace the change needed to propel your life forward and put you on a destiny-bound path. While we all know that change is not easy, it is possible, and more importantly, it's possible to make change last. Despite the discomfort it may cause, change is necessary. If you want a better job, it takes change. If you want more productivity or success in your business, it requires change. If you want to make a greater impact in your ministry or nonprofit, it mandates change. It's been said that "The only thing constant in life is change." Uncomfortable as it may be, regardless of the emotional conflict you experience, change will propel you into seeing your vision and reaching your goals.

Additionally, I will teach you how to lead with your newfound vision and to find that purpose that has been screaming from your heart and hidden beneath the layers of vision blockers. You will gain the skill to redirect your path to the one that lines up with your passion. Overcoming your vision blockers goes beyond just overcoming what stopped you to embracing what will move you forward. Progress is possible, and by following the process, it becomes probable.

Over the past twenty years, I have held several different roles in my career. Pastoring two churches, holding the position of regional manager for a major bank, speaking at leadership conferences all over the world, and working with countless individuals who are just like you and me. From these experiences, I have noticed some patterns—people are facing very similar problems and find themselves stuck for very similar reasons. I have been blessed in my life to have married my high school sweetheart, raised two very strong and independent children, worked with some of the most outstanding people in the world, and learned from some of the greatest professors and mentors life has to offer. Each role I've had has come with a lesson for overcoming a vision blocker or two that tried to keep me from the life I was made to live. Some lessons have been difficult, challenging, and filled with emotion. Throughout this book, you will take a guided tour through the same processes and strategies that have worked so well for so many others, including myself. You will get a glimpse inside some of the difficulties in my life and see some of the amazing lessons I have learned that will help you see your own future much brighter and clearer than ever before.

I have spent countless hours working with individuals, seeing the challenges they faced, and watching them find success—success that I know you can find too. I realize the process of facing some of your deepest, darkest secrets might be a little frightening at first. I also understand you may feel doubt or scared by the risk of feeling vulnerable. Believe me, the risk is worth taking. Within you is the power to be something and someone so great. You have the capacity to live a life so rewarding that books will be written about you. It is normal to be apprehensive and pause before acting; in life, there are times to be cautious. But this isn't one of them. Now is the time for bold action and courage that help you face the very things that have been holding you back for so long. It's time to take the challenge and embrace the journey to overcome your vision blockers.

I challenge you to read this book with an open mind. Be honest with yourself and complete the exercises with integrity and vulnerability. Embrace the concepts and take a chance on living the way you were meant to live. I challenge you to go where you haven't gone before and be the person you never thought you could be.

My goal both in writing this book and in executive leadership coaching is to help you achieve everything your life has designed for you. The truth is that you were created for a purpose, and I would love to help you reach that purpose. I want to help you by becoming your accountability partner, your mentor, coach, or a member of your inner circle who is charged with helping you overcome your vision blockers and remove every obstacle to your destiny.

Are you ready for the journey? Do you have an open mind? Have you put your heart on notice that it's time for you to move forward? If so, then let's start right now!

Dr. Eric Scroggins

PART ONE

Identifying Your Vision Blockers

CHAPTER 1

Seeing Clearly

"It's a terrible thing to see and have no vision."
— Helen Keller

Napoleon Hill said, "Whatever the mind of man can conceive and believe, it can achieve." But what if you can't conceive? To achieve anything in life, you first have to see it deep inside of you. To get what you want out of life, you have to know what you want to accomplish. In fact, over the years, many books, white papers, and leadership classes have been written on the topic of vision. Vision is literally the only thing limiting your life. A well-known anonymous quote says, "We are limited not by our abilities, but by our vision." You can go as far as you can see, so how far can you see? If vision is so imperative, and it is, what could possibly be causing you not to develop yours?

If you were to interview some of the most respected leaders or some of the most prominent businesspeople alive today to find out what was the single most important factor in their success, you would hear about their visions. They would each start to tell about what they imagined long before their companies or organizations materialized and then how they went about fulfilling what was in their hearts. All politicians cast visions during each election period. They are compelled to change the world and make an impact on society, and that all begins with a vision. From Apple to Microsoft and from GM to Toyota, from Republican to Democrat and from local leader to regional business, every success story begins with vision.

So what do you do if you don't have a vision and can't seem to develop one? What is causing the vision you so desperately seek from becoming a reality in you?

Matthew 5:8 provides a basis for unlocking some truths about what is causing your vision to be blocked. The verse says, "Blessed are the pure in heart for they shall see God." By unpacking this verse, we can begin to uncover the vision blockers and the root causes for each. Matthew 5:8 holds the secret to releasing vision.

SETTING THE STAGE

It happened on a mountainside in Galilee somewhere near Capernaum. Jesus had been followed by multitudes of people who were totally intrigued by the miracles, healings, and wisdom that flowed from him. Coming off of one of those miracle moments, Jesus saw a mountainside and found a place to sit, as told in Matthew 5:1. The setting of this scene is so incredibly poignant. The people could sense something awesome was about to happen. Like children intensely anticipating opening gifts at Christmas, the disciples gathered close with the people behind, all sitting in anticipation. The air was thick with expectation! Jesus sat down on the mountainside, taking the position assumed by many a teaching rabbi, and all of a sudden, Jesus began to teach his disciples lessons about proper dynamics and personality traits necessary to lead a successful life. He talked about the poor in spirit; he discussed those who mourn; he praised the meek and celebrated those who hunger and thirst for righteousness; he encouraged the merciful and the peacemakers. Then he pointed out one of the most important truths to help people become destiny bound. He made a profound, yet conditional statement, "You shall see God if you have a pure heart." This statement provides the key to unlock and remove the barriers surrounding your vision. Unwrapping this secret will allow you to accomplish more, see more, and be freer to dream than ever before. Jesus identified the pure heart as the propellant to seeing God and your vision.

Let's take this statement in reverse order to understand properly the reward before we gain clarity on the condition. The second part of this statement, "will see God," tells us that God wants to be noticed, and truthfully, He has an insatiable desire for us to see Him. It's because He knows that when we see God, we see so much more. We see the possibilities of life, we see the purposes of life. We see the world in a whole new and exciting way. More importantly, He wants each person to realize that there is great purpose and design for his or her life. The word "see" in this verse is translated in two different ways. It actually has a duality of meaning. First, it means that you stand before God and meet Him face-to-face. We gain an eternal perspective from that definition. Eternally and eventually, we will stand in His presence and recognize Him as a loving and caring God. Second, it means "to gaze with wide opened eyes as at something remarkable." It's in this meaning that we realize that God has designed each of us to have a vision for our future. To see our lives as part of a greater plan that has great value.

IMPORTANCE OF VISION

Vision gives the heart something to fight for. It provides the fuel and fans the flames that ignite inside of you. Vision has a distinct purpose in focusing your thoughts, your emotions, and your heart on the same objective. Vision is not about sight. It's about that picture you have in your heart that things can change. Not only can they change, but they should change. Vision is that deep-seated emotional drive, the gnawing deep inside that shows you exactly what your life should look like and what your life should accomplish. A life devoid of vision lacks the momentum, enthusiasm, or acceleration to conquer much of anything. Mark Twain said, "I can teach anybody how to get exactly what they want out of life. The problem is that I can't find anybody who knows what they want." Vision tells you what you want. Residing in each of us is this quality that simply needs to be unblocked and released, taking us beyond our current situation.

Today, I'm blessed to be an author, professional speaker, coach, and banker who is driven to lead a life of impact. I dream of touching the lives of people I encounter in such a profound way that they are released from their vision blockers to make great impacts of their own. The life I lead today began with a vision I developed as a teenage boy. I grew up in a fairly middle class family with decent means. Not enough to splurge, but enough to be content. My mom and dad raised four healthy kids who are all fairly well-adjusted and raising great families of their own. Our family was blessed to have Mom home most of the time. After school, we were relegated to homework and chores, and my mother frequently asking, "What do you want to be when you grow up?" While I was a really young boy, I'm sure she was looking for the cute response to share with my aunties. But as I reached adolescence, that question began to take on deep meaning and form something inside me. When I was sixteen and seventeen and in high school, the question gained further significance. "What do you want to be when you grow up?" As I pondered the question, the answer slowly became clear. In fact, as a senior in high school, I wrote a business plan for my life—a set of goals and accomplishments with a set of strategies that I hoped to fulfill. It was, in essence, the formulation of my vision. My vision at that time was filled with optimism and futuristic thinking appropriate for a visionary teenager. It became a living document for my life. After more than twenty-five years, I still have that document and review it from time to time. While my life has taken some interesting detours, what I saw as a teenager I am living today.

This vision has driven me to do things I never would have done otherwise. It caused me to make sacrifices, study more, learn leadership skills, and fight for the things I want in my life. Vision is what makes you get up in the morning and work late into the evening, and it gives you the passion to do what other people won't. It gives you fight and keeps you going. Before you can achieve anything, you have to see it. If you don't see it, you won't achieve it.

VISION EQUIPS YOU FOR BATTLE

Hardly a greater force exists on earth than a man or woman with vision. When you meet someone with vision, you know that person will fight for what he or she sees. S. Truett Cathy is the founder and owner of Chick-Fil-A and no stranger to the fight that vision gives. Chick-Fil-A is a multibillion dollar fast food franchise that was built from meager beginnings, starting with his first restaurant, the Dwarf Grill. Cathy fought one setback after another, including the complete destruction of his second location being overtaken by fire. His business partner was his older brother who was tragically killed in a plane crash, leaving Cathy to go it alone in the food business. Not long after, Cathy was struck by sickness that caused him to be bedridden and unable to work or operate his restaurants.

But during that sickness, the vision for Chick-Fil-A was born. This vision caused Cathy to beat the illness, launch the new franchise, and begin to build one of America's premier fast food chains.

Vision is the catalyst causing you to fight. Conversely, having no vision disqualifies you from battle. Let's look at a story from the Bible that illustrates this point. 1 Samuel 11 tells the story of Nahash the Ammonite coming against God's people:

> Then Nahash the Ammonite came up and encamped against Jabesh Gilead; and all the men of Jabesh said to Nahash, "Make a covenant with us, and we will serve you." And Nahash the Ammonite answered them, "On this condition I will make a covenant with you, that I may put out all your right eyes, and bring reproach on all Israel."

It seems like a very odd request, to put out the right eye of each man in the city. But for a warrior trying to take over a region, it made perfect sense. This action would affect the vision of the men and forever place a badge of slavery upon them, disqualifying them from serving as warriors. At that time, the right eye was necessary for battle because a warrior would need to look over the shield, held in the left hand to protect the body from harm, to see the oncoming enemy. If you can imagine the armor of the day, the shield was held in the left hand and extended from the middle of the body up to the face covering the left side. A soldier would need his right eye to see around the top of the shield. Losing vision in the right eye meant that you were not equipped to fight because you would be an easy target for the enemy. Nahash knew that handicapping Israel this way would cause the men to become complacent and easily conquered.

The same is true for you. Without vision, there is nothing to fight for and our lives become complacent and easily conquered.

What things are you willing to fight for? If you were challenged with a setback, what would cause you to keep going? List the most important things in your life:

_____   _____

_____   _____

_____   _____

THE ABSENCE OF VISION

Proverbs 29:18 says that "without vision the people perish." Having no dream is devastating to life. To perish, according to this verse, means to dissipate, revolt, or become unbridled. It's a definition that can be applied to many lives today. Overwhelmed, chaotic, frustrated, disgruntled, disconnected are all words that describe a person without vision. Often lack of vision is the foundational issue for why you do not have what you want or are not where you want to be. Instead, you are stuck in a dead-end job, irritated with the wages you earn, frustrated with the knowledge that there is more to life than this. If you were to dig deeper, you would find that most of your relationships are also fragmented or strained at best. Every story you tell may even be about a wrongdoing or a desire to "get over" something or take advantage of someone. I saw such stories unfold all too often during my pastorate. I came to realize very quickly (or not so quickly) that my divine assignment was literally eye-opening. What I mean is that my church attracted many people with no vision for their lives or who had lost their visions along the way, and I was assigned to help them find new visions. They were great people, talented people, but life's journey simply had either blocked or stolen their visions.

One day, my church became associated with a family living on the outer edge of stressed. The husband owned a small company and his wife assisted in taking care of the books and managing the company's financial aspects. It became evident to me that every interaction with him was a different iteration of the same story: There isn't enough work, we are strapped for cash, the government is against us, my family isn't supportive, and the employees are not doing the right thing. You can see where I'm going with this. Instead of being fueled to build a great organization that blessed all who were associated with it, he was going through the motions, taking each setback one at a time, relegating his life and his business to perpetual mediocrity and, finally, closure. Each day's conversation with him seemed so familiar. Frustration, chaos, and finally, complete depression and stress developed in his life. He did not have vision; he was operating out of obligation in a business he wasn't happy with and a life he didn't want. The truth is that there wasn't enough work because there was no vision. His family was strapped for cash because there was no vision. The employees wouldn't respond correctly because there was no vision. No one knew where the company was going or why.

Your story may be very similar—as you look around, you find you are nowhere near where you want to be, and that's frustrating. You can't see beyond the current situation, and you don't know which way to go. Finances and the stresses of life make the picture of your life darker. The relationships in your life are strained. If you were honest, you would say that your attitude is bad, and similar to the definition of perish, you want to revolt. So what is keeping you from seeing that vision?

Do you have a story that is similar to that of the company owner above? If you had a blank canvas upon which to draw the perfect business, department, non-profit, or ministry, what would it look like? Take a few minutes and describe it here:

_____

_____

_____

_____

_____

Perhaps your vision is too blocked to see something as specific as a business, department, non-profit or ministry in your future. So write down whatever it is you want for your future, such as a peaceful life, freedom from addiction or illness, a lasting relationship, etc.

_____

_____

_____

_____

_____

CONTAMINATION CAUSES BLINDNESS

Our opening verse has two parts. Matthew 5:8 says, "Blessed are the pure in heart, for they shall see God." We talked about the importance of seeing and having vision. We discussed the fact that God wants you to see and have a future. But the preceding phrase, "Blessed are the pure in heart," holds the key to what keeps us from having that vision.

To understand the root cause of blocked vision, let's examine the two main words in the phrase: "pure" and "heart." To start, we should understand that the heart is where your vision originates. Vision is not formulated in your mind, nor is it what you see with your eyes. Vision is what your heart is being compelled to do.

The image of your life that is residing deep inside you—drawing you, motivating you, and pulling you toward its fulfillment. The heart is amazing—it's not only the organ responsible for physical life by pumping blood throughout your body; it's also responsible for life beyond the physical by pumping vision throughout your consciousness. Next is "pure." The word used here is defined as "without corruption, contamination or hindrance." This definition suggests that when the heart is free from anything that may represent contamination, it is released and empowered to see.

We know through years of research and the testimony of medical journals that a heart free of cholesterol and other plaque-causing substances is healthy and produces a long life. The same is true as it relates to vision. A heart free of contaminants and corruptible components will produce a tremendously healthy vision. Just like plaque blocks the flow of blood through the heart, emotional issues such as pain from your past, disappointment, fear; physical issues such as a healthy lifestyle and relationships; and spiritual issues such as morality, traditionalism, and personal habits and activities keep the vision from flowing through your life.

These vision blockers must be overcome, conquered, and completely removed from our lives. Replacing them with healthy alternatives allows vision to come bombarding through our hearts and puts us on a path to great success and tons of life fulfillment.

SUMMARY

Vision is imperative to moving your life forward and giving you the fuel to fight for what you want. The delay comes from not being able to see that life due to contamination, corruption, or hindrances that are blocking you, consuming you, and overtaking your vision. Removing or detoxifying your life—eliminating the very issues that serve to block your vision—will release that vision in a powerful and exciting way. You don't have to live life seeing but not having vision.

CHAPTER 2

Missing the Mark

"To aim is not enough; you must hit."

— Author Unknown

In the last chapter, we learned about the power of vision and how it equips us for battle. In the absence of vision, people perish, but with vision, people are equipped to live their destinies. Additionally, we introduced the idea that toxins or contaminants can cause a vision never to develop in one's life. Extremely talented people with great gifts can completely miss their destinies and have blocked visions as a result of toxic hearts. The first of these vision-blocking contaminants resides in the choices we make and the activities we are engaged in. Some choices are very healthy and lead to a fruitful and productive life while others detract and degrade the life we want to live. These choices cause us to miss the mark. We can view our life as an arrow that has been fired from a bow with an intended purpose to hit the bull's-eye. Some choices put us on that trajectory while others cause us to miss the mark completely.

In this chapter, we will discuss the first vision blocker, "Missing the Mark," and how to overcome its effects so you can realign and position yourself for laser focus.

WHAT IS THE MARK?

Each of us was created with a common purpose. That purpose is to love God with all of our heart, soul, and mind and to love our neighbor as ourselves. God created each human being with a core fundamental purpose of coming into right relationship with Him and living an honor-filled, righteous, and upright life. Hitting the mark is living a life free from the actions, lifestyle choices, thoughts, and habits that detract from a healthy relationship with God. Throughout the Bible, God eloquently unfolds the plan for living that upright life. From Genesis to Revelation, we see stories of men and women striving to walk that path and live in a way that pleases Him. He cautions us about certain actions that will cause us to stray from that path and deviate from our eternal purpose. So many people who read through the Bible only see a set of rules given by a harsh God that tell you what to do and what not to do. The Bible is not meant to be read that way. It was intended to encourage and instruct each of us to make sound choices for life that will lead us down a path to prosperity and power.

My mother-in-law, Pat, probably offered the best explanation I have heard regarding the Bible's intent for our life. She has been a wonderful mentor for me as I have developed in my relationship with God. I can remember early on having such an insatiable appetite for the things of God and His plan for my life. One night at Bible study, we were discussing the idea that the Bible seemed to be just a strict set of rules, giving the reader an ever-increasing list of do's and don'ts. I was at a place in my early Christian journey where I needed an explanation for everything and wanted to know the why. I was frustrated trying to understand what my daily activities had to do with my overall relationship with God and the health of my life as a whole. Pat's explanation was, "You need to understand that God loves you so much and is trying so desperately to keep you in the palm of His hand, protected and safe. Yet throughout our lives, we passionately try to run to the edge and jump off. The Bible is God's set of directions that helps us to stay squarely in the center of His hand."

When we operate our lives according to those instructions, we hit the mark. When we don't, we miss the mark, which is commonly known as "sin." God, in His loving kindness, wants our life to be blessed, powerful, and full of success. Hitting the mark ensures that happens.

FAILING TO HIT THE MARK

What could be so incredibly devastating about failing to hit the mark? The Bible says in Romans 6:23, "For the wages of sin is death, but the gift of God is eternal life in Christ Jesus our Lord." So often we overlook actions, thoughts, habits, and lifestyle decisions without realizing the long-term effects they have on our vision. This verse can be put another way. The payment you receive for the sin you engage in is to be taken off path and led astray. Sin is a deadly disease, causing damage and destruction to everything it touches, including your heart; ultimately, it affects your vision.

Dr. Caroline Leaf, international best-selling author of *The Gift in You* and *Who Switched Off My Brain?*, writes about the effects of toxic thought. She describes the brain as a series of trees that process brainwave activity related to the types of thoughts you have. In her research, a person who spends countless hours watching Internet pornography has a tree that is black and less active, while a person who has less toxic thoughts and imagery in his mind has a tree that is white and very active. Her research has concluded that toxic thinking can be related to illness, disease, and heart-related conditions. Therefore, I believe, detoxifying your brain, your heart, and your life allows you to live healthier, dream bigger, and accomplish more.

The temptation here is to begin assessing yourself as good or bad—and to believe that bad people won't accomplish anything and good people will. That isn't at all what I am attempting to point out. The issue is what you allow your heart to dwell upon, what you allow your brain to think about, and what you allow your body to engage in that is keeping you from developing a vision to conquer or succeed.

Missing the mark, more formally known as sin, is like a parasite consuming all the resources available to develop your vision. I don't want to point out just one example of sin, but let's take pornography again as an example. The issue here is rarely the simple act of spending time on the Internet searching for skin shots; instead, it is a series of events that leads to complete disregard for time, goals, achievement, or the like. Typically, the person (yes, person—man or woman, both have issues here) is going about his or her normal daily activities when the thought of looking at pornography enters the mind. This thought triggers a prolonged series of images played in the mind, enticing and encouraging the person to engage in some sort of act that will result in a complete erotic experience. What started as a simple (or not so simple) thought becomes fully developed in acting out the routine.

James 1:15 says, "Then, when desire has conceived, it gives birth to sin; and sin, when it is full-grown, brings forth death." The example I just described is rather explicit, but sin, or missing the mark, can be anything that consumes your desire, pulling you away from the wholesome, righteous, honorable living for which you were designed. It starts with a simple desire and develops into full-blown sin that brings forth death. Dead heart, dead relationships, dead Vision!

The *Bible Exposition Commentary* says about this verse:

> This is a negative approach, but it is an important one. James said, "Look ahead and see where sin ends—death!" Do not blame God for temptation. He is too holy to be tempted, and He is too loving to tempt others. God does test us, as He did Abraham (Gen 22); but He does not and cannot tempt us. It is we who turn occasions of testing into temptations. A temptation is an opportunity to accomplish a good thing in a bad way, out of the will of God. Is it wrong to want to pass an examination? Of course not; but if you cheat to pass it, then you have sinned. The temptation to cheat is an opportunity to accomplish a good thing (passing the examination) in a bad way. It is not wrong to eat; but if you consider stealing the food, you are tempting yourself.
>
> We think of sin as a single act, but God sees it as a process. Adam committed one act of sin, and yet that one act brought sin, death, and judgment on the whole human race. James described this process of sin in four stages.
>
> Desire – Deception – Disobedience – Death

Sin becomes the focus and consumes everything—all energy—until there is nothing left for your vision. Are there things in your life that are causing you to miss the mark? Are they consuming more and more of your attention, leaving you visionless and hopeless? Do these things occupy entirely too much time and take you far from the path you believe you should be walking?

Take a minute and write down what they are. Be completely vulnerable and honest as you go through this exercise. What thoughts, actions, habits, or lifestyle choices have you made that are keeping your vision from developing?

_____   _____

_____   _____

_____   _____

_____   _____

CORRECTING YOUR AIM

Whether you are Christian or non-Christian, correcting your aim will involve dealing with the issues (parasites) above that keep your heart contaminated and your vision blocked. So how do we deal with the issues? What is the formula for overcoming sin and creating an atmosphere that allows your vision to develop? It's as simple as ABC: **A**ccept or **A**cknowledge the issue. **B**elieve a resolution exists. **C**onfront the issue. Let me illustrate with a personal story.

When I was in the fifth grade, I was a frail, rather puny kid. I was quite a bit smaller than my fifth grade counterparts, and to make matters worse, I was new to the school. As if my size weren't enough, my lack of confidence in myself made me the perfect target. A perfect target for Eddie Salazar, that is. Eddie was the schoolyard bully I dealt with nearly that entire year. Now that I'm older, I have met countless people with their own Eddie Salazar stories. Anyway, Eddie Salazar was a fellow student at my junior high school. He was a bit bigger than I was, and he always hung around the kids everyone wanted to hang around. For some reason, I became the focus of Eddie's attention each and every day during our lunch hour.

At our school, you were able to engage in any number of schoolyard games during recess. There was tether ball, marbles, catch, socializing on the playground, or my personal favorite, basketball. I wasn't the star of the basketball team by any stretch of the imagination, but I loved a pick-up game at recess with a few of the other guys. Each day about six or eight of us would find a court and a ball, divide the teams, and begin a rather competitive game of hoop. Each day that is until Eddie Salazar got me in his sights. From that point on, he made it his personal mission to attack me on the basketball court, kick me, hit me, steal the ball, and go off playing with the other guys in their own game. For several months, it was the same story. I would get the game started, but ten or fifteen minutes into the game, Eddie would come along and repeat the same harassing activity. It was incredibly frustrating, embarrassing, and consumed all of my attention.

While there are several ways to deal with a bully, the way I dealt with Eddie gives us some insight into how we are going to deal with the parasites of sin that are blocking our vision. One day, I decided to confide in my uncle and tell him about the issue I was having with Eddie. After what seemed like forever relating my plight to my uncle, he said, "Eric, what you are dealing with isn't just an everyday bully; you are dealing with a life lesson that once learned will allow you to take on every challenge you face." He told me, "First, you have to have the courage to accept the idea that you are capable of dealing with the problem. You have to believe in yourself enough to take action, and then you have to confront the problem." He began to work with me every day for two weeks, practicing how I was going to deal with this. He started off by having me make positive confessions about my strength, my capabilities, and my worth. To be honest, it seemed rather hokey to a fifth grader who just wanted Eddie to knock it off. However, I went along with it. Each day, my uncle would ask me, "Who are you? Who is better than you? How strong are you? Who is smarter than you?" It was so interesting that after the first few days of answering the questions, I began to believe that I was much stronger than I started out. Then we progressed into some practice rounds about how I would confront Eddie. We would role-play the activity; my uncle would play Eddie and I would play myself. My uncle would try to take the ball from me, hit me, and kick me, and he told me to react boldly, standing firmly in front of him, and to be prepared to take action. He taught me fighting skills—where and how to punch—in case I really needed to defend myself. After two weeks, he said, "Okay, tomorrow when this situation happens, I want you to take action and deal with Eddie."

I have to be honest that I really believed I was going to have to punch Eddie and help him understand that I was sick and tired of being harassed. Well, when the next day's recess time arrived, we all began our ritual of starting the pick-up game in the gym. Same six or eight guys, basketball, and Eddie. After about ten minutes, Eddie came over to attempt to repeat his very well-rehearsed ritual of kicking, hitting, and taking the ball. This time, however, like a well-trained military soldier, I was ready! When Eddie approached me, I tossed the ball to one of the other guys, and I squared off with Eddie. Chest pushed out, fists clenched, shoulders squared, I was completely ready to engage in the battle of the century. Ironically, the only thing I had to do was stand my ground. Eddie realized I wasn't going to be messed with, and he decided it was in his best interest to change his plan.

To deal with sin, we have to use the same ABCs I used in this schoolyard bully situation. First, you have to accept or acknowledge that the issue is really an issue and that you are capable of dealing with it. Writing them down in the previous section helped you recognize that they exist, but do you acknowledge that they are a problem or the beginning of a problem? Secondly, you have to believe that a resolution exists. This belief can be challenging. It is one thing to recognize that you have a problem, quite another to believe you can defeat it. Thirdly, you have to confess your desire to confront the issue by deciding to leave the behavior.

Simply put, it's time to change your mind, and thereby, change your actions. Acts 3:19 tells us to, "Repent therefore and be converted, that your sins may be blotted out, so that times of refreshing may come from the presence of the Lord." I love this Scripture because it gives the answer to sin, but also the reward for taking the step to correct sin. Repent means to change your mind toward something. At first, you believed it was okay to watch pornography; now you have changed your mind and believe God's word that lust is not healthy. Or to use another scenario, perhaps you previously believed that getting drunk every day was okay, but now you have changed your mind and realized that abusing alcohol leads to all sorts of devastating effects, none of which are part of God's plan for your life. To repent is to change your mind from "your mind" to "God's mind" regarding issues in your life. You can repent concerning overeating, anger, violence, theft, dishonesty, or whatever is keeping you from realizing the vision God has for your life.

The second part of the verse says "be converted." So many times, the belief forms that we simply have to change our minds regarding the issue and that's it. In fact, some Christian circles believe that confession followed by the acceptance of God's forgiveness will do the job. Frankly, there is more to it than that. You have to be converted. The word "converted" means to turn oneself from one set of behaviors to another. Replace what was an issue with what is not an issue. Replace your actions with actions God inspires. Replace your desire with His desire. Replace selfishness with selflessness. To be converted simply means to make a decision not to do what you were previously doing and replace it with correct actions, beliefs, thoughts, or lifestyle choices.

Finally, the reward: "So that times of refreshing will come." Dealing with sin or missing the mark provides the fertile soil where a vision can grow. It creates an atmosphere in your heart that is free from contamination; this atmosphere allows the true desire of your heart to begin birthing your vision. Overcoming sin is a powerful step toward creating a vision-healthy heart.

Let's take some steps to correcting your aim right now. It's a simple as ABC: **A**ccept, **B**elieve, and **C**onfront. On the following lines, we'll take the issues from the previous sections and go through the steps of overcoming them together.

Accept: Make a statement of acknowledgment regarding the issue. For example, "I recognize that _____ is an issue for my life. I accept the fact that continuing to engage in this action is not healthy and will keep me from my true destiny."

_____

_____

_____

_____

Believe: Make a declaration of belief that the situation can change—that God will acknowledge your desire to change. For example, "I believe that God is faithful to absolve me of _____. I am willing to change my ways and believe that God will help me each day to remain strong as I change."

_____

_____

_____

_____

Confront: Make a statement of commitment that you are willing to replace the previous action with a healthy one. For example, "I will not spend countless hours surfing the Internet. I will replace that action with the following _____."

_____

_____

_____

_____

HITTING THE MARK—THE POWER OF DOING RIGHT

What can happen if you do the right thing? Have you ever stopped to imagine what could happen if your life were consumed by doing the right thing? What rewards might there be? What fruit might it produce?

One day as a woman was coming out of a local retail store, she was approached by a homeless man, named Billy Ray Harris, who was panhandling for some coin or cash. In her haste to give the man some money, she accidentally placed her engagement ring in the can. Later that day, Billy Ray discovered that he had received a whole lot more than some coin in his can. What he found rattling around the bottom of his can alongside the coin was a beautiful, very precious diamond ring. You might be thinking what most people would think—Billy Ray had hit the lottery. For many in Billy Ray's situation, this discovery could have been a game changer. Billy Ray stated, "The ring was so big I knew it had to be real and it was expensive." It wasn't until the next day that the owner realized what she had done. She was incredibly upset and began to retrace her steps to find the ring. She found that in her haste, she had accidentally placed this ring in Billy Ray's cup the prior day. She went looking for Billy Ray, and when she found him, she asked whether he remembered her from the previous day. Billy Ray did remember her and returned the ring. He knew the ring's value and said, "I still have character and was raised to do the right thing."

Billy Ray did the right thing. The ring's owner notified local media outlets and began a blog talking about the miracle that is Billy Ray Harris. She also began a fund-raiser to help Billy Ray out of his situation, and several months later, she had raised $191,745 to benefit Billy Ray.

Doing the right thing has rewards; living rightly has rewards. In Billy Ray's case, it meant $191,745, but for you, it means much more. It means doing the right thing—removing sin from your life and replacing it with healthy, God-honoring actions to create a very powerful atmosphere that attracts vision and opportunity. The "right" thing is like a powerful electromagnet that, once plugged in, creates a force that is so great, so powerful that a vision is drawn to it like metal to a magnet.

The human soul has an insatiable appetite for the righteous or "right thing." Matthew 5:6 says, "Blessed are they who hunger and thirst for righteousness for they shall be filled." The stomach has within it a mechanism that signals when food is necessary—that mechanism is hunger. In the absence of food, the body begins to transmit signals directly to the brain, triggering a response to eat. These signals consume all thought, emotion, focus, and attention until that need is met. Hunger experienced in the body from lack of food is identical to the hunger in the soul from a lack of righteousness. Your soul hungers for righteousness. When there is a lack of righteousness, the soul begins to transmit signals and send up flags that it needs to eat. As I stated earlier, toxic thoughts, bad decisions, and poor life choices are all creating an environment of famine for your vision. The soul is sending off flairs that it wants to be fed. It is wanting and yearning for the nourishment of righteousness. The nourishment it needs and feeds upon is right behavior, actions, thoughts, and life choices. Once fed, the soul begins to produce an overflow of vision, provision, emotion, and passion that result in your destiny. The promise for a soul that feasts on righteousness is that it shall be filled. Filled with what? How do you describe a full life? What are the characteristics of being filled?

Being filled represents a life that is content and full of joy—a life that accomplishes exactly what it was meant to and touches others along the way.

A very close friend of mine has touched hundreds of lives. His life now consists of speaking at public and private functions on the topics of gang violence and coming out of the gang lifestyle—topics he is very familiar with. Jesse was the leader of one of the largest gangs in southern California from the time he was fourteen. Having had the misfortune of being raised in a tough community with tough circumstances and tough surroundings, he was almost certain to end up in a gang or start one. From the ages of fourteen to sixteen, Jesse was doing things most people would find incomprehensible, yet those things were a way of life for him. Ultimately, Jesse ended up in a very sticky situation, facing time in jail and a conviction for attempted murder and other crimes. About that time, Jesse was introduced to a very different way of living, thinking, and believing. He met Pastor Ruben, a man with vision, heart, compassion, and the tenacity to do the right thing and love people everywhere. Jesse was overwhelmed by the love and support he received from Pastor Ruben, so he couldn't help but be attracted to this new life. Together, they prayed for the outcome of his legal situation and for Jesse to receive mercy and grace from his prosecutors. Jesse was not incarcerated for his actions, which only confirmed the benefits of his new way of living. He then set out to remove all of the old and horrible things from his life and put himself on a new trajectory to accomplish more with a better outcome. That all happened years ago; now Jesse pastors a thriving church and has in turn rescued hundreds of people from very similar situations. He frequently speaks at schools to help prevent young people from choosing gangs as an answer. He gives hope to the hopeless and has traveled to many countries sharing his story. Jesse lives the life now that he could only dream about when his life was consumed with sin.

Jesse's life has been rewarded for making the choice to stop failing to hit the mark and starting to hit the bull's-eye.

Stop to imagine for a moment what you would like to see happen in your life when you make the decision to remove poor choices and replace them with good ones. The Bible says of God, "He is a rewarder of those who diligently seek Him." (Hebrews 11:6) Understanding that God represents righteousness, what would your reward look like? What can you see yourself doing or how would you be living?

Take a moment to imagine your life without sin and describe what it might look like.

_____

_____

_____

_____

_____

_____

_____

RE-AIMING YOUR LIFE

How do you develop an appetite for doing the right thing? A life that has spent years focused on poor choices, bad behaviors, toxic thoughts, or poor life decisions has built a diet containing those very things. The key is to take a taste. Psalm 34:8 in the Bible says, "Oh, taste and see that the Lord is good." An appetite for the Lord is an appetite for righteousness, and it starts with one taste.

In 2000, the movie *Pay It Forward* was released, starring Helen Hunt, Kevin Spacey, and Haley Joel Osment. The story is about a young man charged with producing a social studies assignment involving changing people. The class has to think of a simple way to make the world a better place. Trevor, played by Haley Joel Osment, comes with an experiment and puts his plan in motion. The plan is to do one simple random act of kindness, and instead of being repaid, the recipient has to pay it forward to someone else. The acts of kindness end up reaching all across the country with everyone doing one random act of kindness. Trevor's theory is that if people will do one thing better, the world will be a better place.

The same is true with you and me. The key to re-aiming your life and hitting the mark is to start with something you weren't doing yesterday and start doing it today. One thing! What is the one thing I know I need to stop today so I can start doing the right thing in its place?

Maybe you have an uncontrollable habit of telling lies. Your stories are always fabricated and you aren't truthful, even with the people close to you. Start today by making the decision that your life will be defined by truth and honesty. You are removing the habit of lying and replacing it with telling the truth. Start with one truth! Set your mind on the one thing you are going to talk about or correct. I realize there is risk associated with this activity. The person you have been lying too may get angry, disappointed, or worse, but the truth is that "The truth will set you free" (John 8:32). You will be amazed by how light you feel and how clear your focus becomes when you are truthful. This is only one example of taking a taste of righteousness. Find your own, whatever it happens to be; it's your story and you can tell it the way you want. The important thing is that you begin to find the righteousness in your life and begin implementing a strategy to have righteousness define your life. Later in Chapter 10, we will be dealing with "Making Lasting Change." But right now, make the decision to do one thing differently. No more sin, no more dishonesty, no more toxic thinking, no more destructive choices. You are going to put on righteousness and it will become the new you. Your soul will be fed and your life will take on new direction, allowing your heart's vision to develop.

Write it down: What is the one thing you will start doing differently today? Take a moment and write down the behavior you plan to start right now. Don't wait; make the change now. You will be amazed by how this one thing will begin to feed your soul and change your thinking.

_____

_____

_____

_____

SUMMARY

Activities we decide to engage in, thoughts we have, and habits we can break are all causing us to miss the mark and be less productive than we should and could be. Each one has a way of misdirecting our aim and puts our life a bit out of balance. There is hope to re-aim, redirect, and realign our decisions to create an atmosphere of success and freedom. Doing the right thing and acting according to a righteous standard with honesty and integrity will propel us from our current frustrated position to one of power, authority, and prosperity.

CHAPTER 3

Conquering Strife

"Peace is not merely a distant goal that we seek, but a means by which we arrive at that goal."

— Martin Luther King, Jr.

In the last chapter, I talked about doing the right thing and re-aiming your life so you are always hitting the mark. You were able to identify some things that cause you to miss the mark and make some commitments to eliminate those things from your life. In this chapter, we are going to deal with the vision blocker of strife. If strife is not overcome, it can derail your life for decades, leaving you without vision, without purpose, and without opportunities.

The dictionary defines strife as vigorous or bitter conflict, discord, or antagonism. Further clarity of the term is described as quarreling, rivalry, wrangling, debate, provocation, or factions. Strife is usually at work just below the surface, weaving its way into various parts of your life. In fact, most people don't even realize that this vision blocker is at work, causing chaos and confusion and keeping your focus off your real purpose.

EXPOSING STRIFE

Have you ever met someone who seems irritated all the time? No matter the time of day, who the person is with, or what he is doing, something irritates him. He seems to be living to create contention, constantly carrying discord and quarrels with him everywhere he goes. Maybe the person you know is you. All of your relationships are strained and fragmented by the anger that comes from you. You don't like what is happening in your life, but truly, the only thing you know is to be angry, mad, irritated, and to engage in conflict. When you are living a life to create contention, intentional or unintentional, a vision cannot materialize. Strife pulls all the energy away from your vision and redirects that energy to causing problems for everyone else. Hebrews 12:14-15 says, "Pursue peace with all people, and holiness [oddly, holiness or pureness was our first vision blocker], without which no one will see the Lord."

We already established in the first chapter that to "see the Lord" was synonymous with seeing your destiny or purpose. This passage from Hebrews says that in order to see your future or destiny, you must pursue peace, not contention, not strife, and not quarreling. It is amazing how the same people, who always have a problem with everyone around them and constantly bicker with others and are usually complaining, are the ones who are never on track to do anything of significance, typically are in a state of financial crisis, and have zero direction.

There is a story in Genesis 13:5-11 that details the issues related to strife:

> Lot also, who went with Abram, had flocks and herds and tents. Now the land was not able to support them, that they might dwell together, for their possessions were so great that they could not dwell together. And there was strife between the herdsmen of Abram's livestock and the herdsmen of Lot's livestock. The Canaanites and the Perizzites then dwelt in the land.

So Abram said to Lot, "Please let there be no strife between you and me, and between my herdsmen and your herdsmen; for we are brethren. Is not the whole land before you? Please separate from me. If you take the left, then I will go to the right; or, if you go to the right, then I will go to the left." And Lot lifted his eyes and saw all the plain of Jordan, that it was well watered everywhere (before the Lord destroyed Sodom and Gomorrah) like the garden of the Lord, like the land of Egypt as you go toward Zoar. Then Lot chose for himself all the plain of Jordan, and Lot journeyed east. And they separated from each other.

In this story, strife existed between the men of Abram and the men of Lot. They were arguing, bickering, and causing problems. Abram and Lot were on a journey to prosperity and a new land when this arguing started. We can only surmise that the men were quarreling over worldly prosperity, personal gain, and territorialism as both flocks were occupying the same grazing land. Strife was destroying the progress and relationships between the family members and their followers. Abram realized that no forward progress could be made while the men were fighting. They were totally consumed by the bickering rather than the greater purpose of reaching the prosperous land. Abram approached Lot and said, "Let there be no strife between us." In other words, "Let's make peace and realize that we are in the same family and have the same goal in mind. We both want to succeed, we both want new territory, and we can work collaboratively to achieve our goal."

Strife is evil. It is grounded in a selfish spirit that is fed by jealousy and greed. Proverbs 28:25 says, "He who is of a proud heart [some translations say "greedy"] stirs up strife." You can see the mission of strife to break down relationships and cause division everywhere it is present. Where parents are arguing with their children and children are disrespecting their parents, strife is present. Where husbands are fighting with their wives and wives are angry with their husbands, strife is present. Where coworkers are bickering and arguing, strife is present. Strife causes fractionalization of relationships and results in depression, anxiety, and pain.

Strife's effects were never more evident than in one of the offices I was assigned to as a bank manager. When I arrived as the new manager, I was met with some of the most talented and knowledgeable staff in the business. In fact, in all my years as a banker, I had rarely worked with such a skilled team. It was evident that each individual was passionate about his or her job and committed to the company's success. As a result, I wasn't really prepared for what I encountered over the next several weeks. I knew the role I needed to fill and how to drive the business to our company, and I proceeded to develop a plan to do just that. The banking business is built on customer service and developing relationships with clients, prospects, and coworkers that result in a growing business and a profitable branch. Each day, I would come to work with a childlike optimism; unfortunately, each day I was met with story after story of coworker issues, backstabbing, quarreling, territorialism, and conflict. On days when there were no stories, the branch atmosphere was frigid and silent. I realized quickly that my team members did not like each other, only tolerated the working conditions of being in the same office with each other, and they were definitely going to protect their territory. Strife was running rampant like a plague through a small community, each day killing more and more of the hope and vision that this office could be a top contender in the community and the company. The issues of strife were so bad that when temporary employees filled in on days we were shorthanded, they would leave with no desire to return. The effects of strife on this office were very real and tangible. There was very little passion to succeed as a team, and virtually no vision to move forward, so production was rarely the focus.

To overcome strife, you have to be honest with yourself and realize that the person causing the problems, starting the fights, and creating the chaos in your life is the person you look at in the mirror every day: YOU! Can you identify relationships in your life where strife exists? Are you willing to identify areas of anger, frustration, and quarreling that you cause?

Take a few minutes and write down the names of the people you quarrel with the most. Think back over the last thirty days to situations in which anger, quarreling, or fighting occurred and write them down.

People   Relationship to Me (e.g. sibling, parent, coworker)

_____   _____

_____   _____

_____   _____

_____   _____

Situations that have occurred where strife exists:

1. _____
2. _____
3. _____
4. _____
5. _____

BLESSINGS OF A PEACEMAKER

What is a peacemaker? How is peace related to my vision? Doesn't being a peacemaker make me a weak person? Matthew 5:9 says "Blessed is the Peacemaker…" Note that Christ did not say, "Blessed is the peace giver or blessed are the peaceful." He said the peacemaker or one who makes peace.

A peacemaker is not a person devoid of fight or drive or someone who in some way should be described as weak. In fact, peacemakers are some of the most passionately driven people you will encounter. A case in point is Mother Teresa, winner of the Nobel Peace Prize for her work in India with the less fortunate and abandoned. When she spoke, she did so with conviction and with passion to eradicate the injustices done to the orphans of India. Her words were direct and invoked a response from all who listened. While she was loving, caring, and a promoter of peace, one could argue that she was also a fighter.

Another example of how the fight is placed squarely on the shoulders of the peacemaker is Dr. Martin Luther King. He was a man who fought against the injustices of racial segregation and fought for the equal rights of all men. Written in the text of his famous "I Have a Dream" speech are the powerful words: "We must forever conduct our struggle on the high plane of dignity and discipline. We must not allow our creative protests to denigrate to physical violence. Again and again we must rise to the majestic heights of meeting physical force with soul force." While he was a fighter for sure, he only supported demonstrations that were founded in peace and he would not allow them to result in physical altercations at any cost.

A grave difference exists between a pacifier and a peacemaker. Pacifiers simply try to smooth things over and cover them up instead of dealing with them. A peacemaker is driven to create peace wherever he or she finds quarreling by confronting and addressing the issues at hand. Peacemakers are skilled at dealing with different types of people in different situations. They make peace out of chaos. I believe Christ said, "Blessed is the peacemaker" because it emulated his purpose on this earth. He said, "I came to seek and to save that which is lost." Like other peacemakers, his total focus was on others, not on himself.

There is a story of two gentlemen in a community who were constantly at odds with one another. Both John and Fred had absolutely zero tolerance for the other, and they were forever engaged in a game of one-upmanship, attempting to outdo the other. One day, a peacemaker entered the scene; he had to do business with both men, and he realized the tension, stress, and discomfort this situation placed on all involved. While having a conversation with John, the peacemaker asked, "What do you think about Fred?" Not surprisingly, John had nothing but terrible things to say about Fred and went on to say, "Everyone knows that I can't stand Fred." The peacemaker responded, "Sure, but you have to admit Fred is a hardworking individual." John said, "Well, no one can deny how hard Fred works." The next time the peacemaker saw Fred, he told him, "Do you know what John said about you?" Fred responded, "You can't believe John's lies." The peacemaker said, "Well, he said he doesn't know a harder working person." "He said that?" Fred was stunned. "What do you think about John?" asked the peacemaker. Fred replied, "It's no secret that I have absolutely no use for him." "But you must admit he is an honest businessman?" asked the peacemaker. "Well, sure, in business you can always trust John," Fred responded. Later that week, the peacemaker had reason to see John and asked him, "Do you know what Fred said about you?" "No telling," John responded with a snort. The peacemaker said, "He claims that in business you are absolutely someone to trust." "What do you know about that?" John responded with a smile. A couple of weeks later, John and Fred were giving a kind nod to each other, and several weeks after that, they were shaking hands and having meals at each other's homes.

Peacemakers make peace! The peacemaker's blessings lie in the focus of his or her actions. While strife is selfish and promotes personal interests, peacemakers spend their days focusing on the interests of others. Let's talk about the blessings that come from this worthwhile attribute.

Blessing 1—Human Reconciliation: Peacemakers are responsible for reconciliation among human beings. Their focus is to create unity and harmony among the human race. Peacemakers envision relationships restored and people working in harmony. You can see how vision can thrive in this environment. Often, the vision for our life revolves around creating a better world and better relationships.

What relationships in your life need to be reconciled?

_____

_____

What actions could you take today to begin that reconciliation?

_____

_____

How did taking that action make you feel?

_____

_____

Blessing 2—Generosity of Spirit: Peacemakers set the standard for giving to others. Peacemakers are constantly on the lookout for ways to give to the public good. In fact, peacemakers believe that their own self-interests are advanced in the advancement of others' interests. Whether it's giving to better the human condition, eliminating human suffering, or creating a place of refuge for the lost, no matter what the cause, peacemakers have one; they fight for their causes and give everything they have to move their missions forward. Many people believe that giving money is the only thing that counts as giving. The truth is that peacemakers find three ways to give:

1. **Time:** Giving hours of service to a cause can change the entire atmosphere of an organization and you for that matter. When you give your time, you become personally invested in the mission. Not only are you lending a hand to complete a task, but you are taking personal ownership in the mission; it becomes part of your story and part of your life.

2. **Talent:** Giving skills that you possess allows two things to take place: 1) The organization or effort becomes stronger because you are filling a vital need. For instance, if your talent is leadership, then you can help the organization operate more efficiently or help to provide motivation and direction to the volunteers. In my own life, I serve on the board of several organizations. My skills are in financial management and leadership, so I find places that are in need of those skills and begin to use them to move forward the organization's mission. Maybe you are not a leader, and the only skill you have is in packing boxes or filing papers. These skills are so vital to an organization. Find an organization in your community and ask it whether you can come help file papers or pack boxes and you will be amazed by the astonishment on their faces. In every community, so many worthwhile efforts exist—places in desperate need of help and assistance. Find those places and give your talent. 2) Your vision begins to develop out of your service. When you begin giving of what you can do, you will be amazed by how you begin to change and your vision begins to come clear. This generosity of spirit creates a fertile field for vision to be planted and grow. Often vision is birthed in seeing

that something needs to change and being willing to give of yourself to make that change.

3. **Resources:** Money is also very important to advance any organization's mission. Recently, I was introduced to the A21 campaign (www.A21campaign.org), an organization whose mission is to eradicate human trafficking around the world. A21 has set up safe houses, rescue workers, lawyers, ex-military and law enforcement workers, administrators, and leaders throughout the globe. This movement is necessary and very important to the human condition around the world. It also is very expensive to operate, requiring approximately $20 million annually. Giving your money to causes like A21 allow you to become part of the mission. It's understandable that many of us can't go around the world and help with causes and efforts, but each of us can give something to help those who do. When you begin to invest your money in giving to create peace, it becomes part of your life and begins to transform your heart. Remember, "Those who are pure in heart will see...."

What cause are you giving to?

_____

_____

Are you giving time, talent, or resources?

_____

_____

What skill do you possess that could be offered?

_____

_____

List efforts or organizations to which you could give of yourself:

_____

_____

Blessing 3—Strength and Conviction: Peacemakers have strength to challenge the status quo and conviction actually to take action. Instead of fanning flames of strife and contention, peacemakers use their influence and wisdom to reconcile contending parties, adjust their differences, and restore them to a state of unity. To accomplish this requires strength and conviction that goes beyond thoughts of "what should be done" to thoughts of "what must be done." Peacemakers are world changers who have strength that lives deep down in their souls, compelling them to make change regardless of personal attacks, opinions, or contradictions. You can see why vision will live in this atmosphere. However, having a conviction that compels you to move the needle on life and having a vision that must be fulfilled will lead to opposition from many people. Nevertheless, peacemakers are stronger than the opposition and have a deeper conviction that will stand against those who say, "No" or "It can't be done." Peacemakers know it must be done.

Look around your world—what do you see that must be changed—something that you know from the bottom of your heart is not right and must be addressed?

_____

_____

FOUR KEYS FOR GETTING ALONG

Strife continues to divide, separate, and destroy relationships. Husbands are at odds with their wives, wives are battling with their husbands, children fight with their parents, and parents argue with their children. However, families are not the only area of relation-ship issues affected by strife. You see friends moving apart, cowork-ers working against one another, church members fighting, organi-zation volunteers irritated. Where strife is present, relationships are at risk and vision is nowhere near developing, unless the vision is to eliminate strife. Look at the relationships in your life and around you—do you see anything similar to what I have just described? Further, are you the person at the center of it all? Do you make it your life's mission to create drama that pits people against each other? While that may sound a bit dramatic, the question really is: Are you doing anything to get along with others and help them get along with each other? How are you interacting with others, and do you have the ability to reconcile relationships to make them productive?

Four keys exist for getting along with others. These keys will help you create some of the greatest relationships you have ever experi-enced. These keys are the enemy of strife, and once implemented into your daily life, they will eradicate strife so vision can emerge.

Key #1: Change Your Words, Change Your Life

Getting along with others begins with great communication and what comes out of your mouth. An old proverb says, "Kind words are like honey—sweet to the taste and good for your health." All too often, relationships and teams fall apart or break down because of terrible communication or words that are not thought out before spoken. Relationship problems often can be eliminated by simply changing the way you speak to others and how you communicate. Things you say either elicit trust or break it down. We all know that trust is foundational to good relationships and is fostered when people know you care about them and are concerned about what goes on in their lives. As soon as people think you are motivated for yourself rather than for them, alarms are set off inside them, telling them to watch out for you. Trust begins to break down and the relationship deteriorates. Kind words begin to flow when you are empathetic to the people in your life and those you encounter on a daily basis. My wife is an expert in this area. She is constantly seeing things from others' viewpoints and choosing her words carefully so as not to offend. Saundra can quickly assess others' feelings and gain a clear perspective on their viewpoints. Her words are always chosen with care and spoken to build up and encourage whomever she speaks to. Saundra embodies the idea that "kind words are like honey" because people are attracted to her words and drawn into relationships with her largely due to how she communicates with them. Masterful!

I discussed earlier a bank branch to which I was assigned where the staff members' relationships were extremely strained. One area I focused on to resolve this issue was how the team communicated. I no longer tolerated speaking ill of a coworker or complaining about others' performances, workloads, or lack thereof. The new rule was that we were going to operate like a team and speak well of each other; we would build up each other and look out for one another. Changing the communication alone created an atmosphere of success and camaraderie that was so attractive to others that when an opening became available, a line of potential candidates desired to fill the spot.

Communication is key—change the words you say and make them kind!

Key #2: Be Friendly, Even When You Don't Feel Like It

Being friendly goes way beyond adding someone to your Facebook account and calling yourself friends. You would think that being friendly was a relatively easy concept, yet in our digital, media-driven, Facebook friends, Twitter-based world, being friendly has become increasingly difficult. Being friendly is defined as being attached to another person by feelings of affection or personal regard; giving assistance or support to another person; showing kindness toward or being helpful to another person. The characteristics of being friendly are about how you treat other people: showing them affection or personal regard, caring for them, and being concerned about their wellbeing. Strife is not interested in these characteristics, and therefore, showing them kindness will eliminate it from your life.

A national news story told about two girls on opposite teams doing something remarkable. Meghan and Arden were competing in the 3200 meter race at the high school championships in Ohio. At the end of the race, Arden was leading Meghan when she began to collapse on her way to the finish line. Instead of passing her, Meghan decided to pick her up and assist her to the finish line, so they crossed together. These two opponents, each competing for her own place in the championships, gave us a wonderful example of being friendly. When interviewed, Meghan told reporters that she credits her parents for teaching her that people are more important than anything else. It was natural for her to see a struggling opponent and decide to pick her up instead of leaving her behind.

This action by Meghan shows us how friendship and being friendly can change life's circumstances. Meghan and Arden were opponents, but now they are best friends. Being friendly is about caring for another person—setting your mind and your heart to reach out and treat others kindly with care and compassion.

Key #3: Forgive

I will discuss forgiveness in Chapter 7, "Healing Pains from Your Past," but I want to mention here that relationships are strained, the future is stunted, and vision is impossible when you can't forgive. When we harbor anger, frustration, vengeance, and retaliation against people who have hurt us, and we do not forgive them, we only hurt ourselves further.

A lack of forgiveness begins to form bitterness, and bitterness forms anger, and anger forms hatred, which ultimately kills any vision. Forgiveness is not your acceptance of a wrongdoing or forgetting what has happened; it is simply a releasing of that person in your heart from the retribution you believe he or she is due. By allowing someone's actions against you to have a safe harbor in your heart, you tie yourself to that person emotionally and mentally. For instance, let's say a young boy has been abused by someone in his life (an all too often occurrence in our world). Once that boy grows into a man, he will try to become part of society in a productive manner, but if he is holding onto anger, frustration, embarrassment, and contention for his abuser, it will cause his relationships to be shallow and unfulfilling. Men attempt to compartmentalize and put emotions in a box or out of their minds, and they can mask those feelings for quite some time. But issues begin to materialize when intimacy with a spouse enters the scene. Over and over, stories are told of men in similar situations who are unable to adjust, unable to commit, unable to develop deep relationships with friends or spouses, all related back to the abuse suffered as a child. To forgive the abuser does not mean that the abuser is justified in his or her actions. It does not mean that the young boy accepts what happened as valid or acceptable, and it does not absolve the abuser from the consequences of those actions. Forgiveness allows the man to free his heart, mind, and soul from holding on to that boyhood pain and keeping it at the forefront of his experiences.

Forgiveness releases you to develop deep relationships with others and allow people into your world. Forgiveness draws people close while a lack of forgiveness keeps them apart.

Key #4: Eliminate Gossip

Everyone loves a juicy story until the juicy story is about him. Over the years, I have seen gossip destroy more relationships and break down more teams than I care to count. Proverbs 21:23 says, "Whoever guards his mouth and tongue keeps his soul from trouble." When you engage in gossip, you affect the reputation of the person you are talking about, spreading stories that may or may not be true, and you destroy any trust in the relationship. Furthermore, people who engage in gossip usually do it to build themselves up. However, if you are viewed as a gossiper, people will think that you will gossip about anyone, including them, and that only destroys their trust in you.

To get along with people and eliminate strife, you must set a very hard and fast policy in your life that gossip will not be tolerated. It is amazing how easy it is to eliminate gossip when you set your heart upon it. Here are some steps to begin:

- Have a policy that when someone around you begins to tell you a story about someone, you will quickly change the subject.
- Decide that information you hear is for your benefit only and not to be repeated.
- Let all of your conversation regarding others serve to build them up and not tear them down.
- Remove yourself from the conversation—just walk away.

When you set the standard that gossip is not for you, you will be shocked how fast you can make friends and deepen relationships.

By implementing these Four Keys: Change Your Words, Be Friendly, Forgive, and Eliminate Gossip, you have a strategy for getting along with people and conquering strife in your life.

REDIRECTING THE ENERGY

What do you do with all the energy that was previously focused on causing strife? Causing strife and maintaining a focus on chaos and contention requires a massive amount of physical, emotional, and spiritual effort. That effort can be redirected into more productive and useful areas of your life. Vision is produced once you decide that you will no longer allow strife to govern your actions, thoughts, and relationships.

Author and speaker Joyce Meyer tells the story about her early years living in a very angry and frustrated state. She was abused, married the wrong person who perpetuated the abuse, struggled to raise her children, was neglected, and totally passed off as nothing. She was an angry person who had very little good to say to anyone. She was quick with her tongue and could cut even the sharpest person down in a moment of time. But as her relationship with the Lord grew stronger, she desperately sought peace. Living her life angry and frustrated was causing her children to disrespect her and repeat to her the same things she was shouting at them. She began to learn the blessings of a peacemaker, how to get her anger and strife under control, and eventually, to eliminate it altogether. Today, Joyce Meyer's ministry and teachings affect millions of people every year. She is a world-renowned author, speaker, and teacher, respected for her no-nonsense approach to the Word of God.

Joyce redirected her anger to peace and her energies to helping people around the world by spreading a message of hope, love, and strength. All the energy she was using to be angry and frustrated is now redirected toward good.

Notice that Joyce's transformation started with a desire for peace, then worked into how she could get her anger under control, and then she redirected her efforts to something positive. The same is true with you and me. As a first step, we must want the change and desire the peace; then we need to begin working on determining and stopping the actions that perpetuate the strife in our lives, and then redirect that energy to something positive.

What positive things can you do? What can you redirect your energy to that will make a difference in your life and the lives of others? Thousands, even millions of opportunities exist to redirect the energy you previously directed toward strife into something positive: Kids in every community need food, clothing, and shelter; nearly every city is dealing with a homeless population; counseling centers need compassionate, caring individuals to volunteer, as do drug abuse clinics and troubled youth centers. Volunteering could be something as simple as reading a book to an elementary school student in your local neighborhood. The point is to find something positive that you are passionate about and redirect your energies toward it.

Take a minute and brainstorm ten efforts in your community that may need assistance. You may even come up with a few other activities—like bringing flowers to your wife at work once a week. Take a minute and write them down:

_____   _____

_____   _____

_____   _____

_____   _____

_____   _____

Once you have them written down, take some time to decide which one you will start today.

HARNESSING THE POWER

Where did all this influence come from? That's the question you will be asking once you have dedicated your life to eliminating strife and focusing on peace. With that influence comes the obligation to do more good and affect more people for good. It is amazing how peacemakers begin to gain influence all over the world and then affect change in companies, organizations, ministries, and neighborhoods everywhere. The key is to understand the power that comes with becoming a peacemaker and harnessing it toward your vision.

Mother Teresa spent most of her adult life working in and operating orphanages in Calcutta, the poorest part of India. There wasn't a child she wouldn't take; in fact, when she addressed the U.S. Congress at the National Prayer Breakfast, she said, "Stop killing the babies. Give them to me; I will take them." She spent her life making peace for troubled children, helping families who would abandon children, caring for the poor by feeding them, bringing people medicine and caring for them when they were sick. She sacrificed her life for the benefit of others and was respected by millions and millions of people for doing so. Mother Teresa used her influence to raise money, love people, and change the way nations addressed the poor's needs. She harnessed that power to influence humanity and cause us all to evaluate our own lives very closely and ask what we can do to change the lives of others. Many of Mother Teresa's recorded quotes are related to loving one another, speaking well of one another, and smiling at each other. Her message of hope and inspiration has changed the lives of so many. Mother Teresa used her influence to bring people from all over the world to her doorstep so she could communicate the tragedy facing children in India. Reporters, medical professionals, photographers, and historians would all come to her orphanage to record the work being done and witness the remarkable transformation taking place in the children's lives.

When you become a peacemaker, people will be attracted to you and your cause. Your vision will begin to materialize inside of you, and as you begin working on projects or commit to efforts that change people or in some way serve humanity, that vision will draw support, resources, and connections to you that will allow your vision to take on a life of its own.

Harnessing the power of this newfound influence requires four fundamental areas of focus:

1. **Communication:** A peacemaker is apt to listen to others. Over the years, I have taken many business training classes to help with sales, relationship building, presentation, and closing the deal. Each class contains a component that deals with listening skills and the power of hearing others. All too often, we are talking instead of listening, which tells others that we are more concerned with our own thoughts, emotions, feelings, and ideas than theirs. Communication is key; however, listening is the component of communication that tells others how important they are to you. When you are leading others, developing new relationships, or relating to your family, the most powerful action you take is to listen. In today's society, everyone is talking and very few are listening. As a peacemaker, you won't know how to help unless you can listen.

2. **Relationships:** As I stated earlier, strife looks to break down relationships, cause chaos and contention, and undermine others. As a peacemaker, your new responsibility is to seek out relationships and find ways to make them strong. People are the most important part of any life. As I have said for years, "People are more important than the Project," or "The Worker is more important than the Work." Up to this point, strife may

have been the cause of strained relationships in your life or fights among you and your siblings. Your children may resent you or your spouse may have difficulty getting along with you. Maybe your coworkers simply tolerate being around you. That is all about to change. You are now a peacemaker who values the relationships in your life above all. Today, you go to work to mend those relationships by apologizing to those with whom you have been angry, offering to go to coffee with others who have been at odds with you, or inviting others over for tea. In any event, the time is now to begin mending broken relationships and forming new ones. Peacemakers are always on the lookout for hurting, broken people, and they are compelled to make a difference in those people's lives.

3. **Opportunities:** Since we are talking about vision blockers and strife is one of them that consumes all of your energy, it stands to reason that you have not been particularly aware of opportunities that have come your way. Strife is evil because it consumes and misdirects your focus from opportunity to chaos. As a peacemaker, you are going to be on high alert for new opportunities that come into your life so you are ready to seize them. The effort you previously placed on causing strife will be redirected to seizing opportunities that align with your passion. I know from my own life that listening to others and focusing on relationships has brought me many opportunities to succeed. As a business development manager, I spend most of my days finding ways to impact my community positively. Whether it's volunteering at a homeless shelter, leading an economic development organization, or collecting donations for the hungry, this level of service brings opportunities to expand my business. I am poised to grow my business because I am positioned to help others.

4. **Action Orientation:** Peacemakers take action. Nothing happens in your life until you are willing to move. Strife-oriented people are focused on causing chaos, exposing others to their own frustrations, and perpetuating contention into others' lives. They never take action on positive, productive, progress-oriented projects. This isn't so with peacemakers. As I stated earlier, the nature of a peacemaker is to feel compelled to bring reconciliation to others—to bring compassion and love to broken and desperate relationships. Think about the story of Fred and John I told earlier; the peacemaker was compelled to reconcile that relationship. What are you compelled to do? You must take action and be ready to move on the opportunities that are presented in your life. Your vision will develop when you begin moving forward and taking advantage of what develops before you. Take action!

SUMMARY

Strife is an evil underneath the surface of your life. Its mission is to destroy relationships, progress, and most importantly, your vision. Where strife exists, there are contentions and every evil work. Strife is like a virus that eats away at every part of you until you are left with nothing but bitterness and loneliness, which is nowhere near the purpose for which you were designed. That purpose is Peace!

Strife is counteracted by peace, and peacemakers are the instigators of that change. Becoming a peacemaker allows your life to be overrun with blessings and a power you never dreamed could be possessed. Those blessings lie in the actions we take to create peace in our world and create a formidable atmosphere for your vision to begin developing. They are blessings of human reconciliation, generosity of spirit, strength, and conviction. Become a peacemaker and take part in the blessings that will change your world.

CHAPTER 4

Unifying the Mind

"Lack of direction, not lack of time, is the problem.
We all have twenty-four-hour days."

— Zig Ziglar

Chapter 3 was all about how we treat others and the crippling effects strife can have on your life and on the development of your vision. Hopefully, you took advantage of the opportunity to look at the various relationships in your life and how you are bringing value to or breaking down those relationships. I challenged you to bring the blessings of a peacemaker to your life by changing some things about the way you think and act toward humanity. In this chapter, we are going to look at the way you treat your own life. Often our own abilities get in the way of our true calling, so we spend too much time on too many things, none of which get us to our destiny. The vision blocker of double-mindedness is a trap that gives the appearance of success but never delivers the kind of results that can be achieved by walking in your one true passion.

THE DOUBLE-MINDED MAN

James 1:6-8 says, "But let him ask in faith, with no doubting, for he who doubts is like a wave of the sea driven and tossed by the wind. For let not that man suppose that he will receive anything from the Lord; he is a double-minded man, unstable in all his ways." This passage refers to a man who needs wisdom to navigate his life, so he is searching for who or what can provide it for him. Doubt begins to creep in, probably based on varying opinions of where that wisdom originates. Apparently, he is looking everywhere and anywhere only to find himself without what he was seeking. The man is described as double-minded, meaning he is unfocused, inconstant, wavering, going in too many directions at the same time, or traveling between popular opinions and never settling on one conviction.

This world is full of opinions, sides of issues to take, personal interests, hobbies, opportunities, clicks, special interest groups, outside activities, inside activities, career paths, jobs you can take, promotions you can get, industries you can create, humanitarian groups you can support, religions you can choose, convictions you can follow, countries where you can live, cities where you can move. And if that weren't enough, there is Google, Bing, Twitter, Facebook, LinkedIn, Pinterest, Flickr, Tumblr, Instagram, and so on, all of which are vying for your time and your focus. All of it can be so overwhelming. It isn't surprising that we are blocked in our vision by being double-minded when we are presented with so many things from so many different outlets all communicating with us at once. The issue is that the double-minded man or woman gets caught up in those distractions and never settles on the one area that will propel him or her to life's blessing. A double-minded man or woman, by definition, is unstable in all his or her ways.

We will focus on two components of double-mindedness in this chapter. First, double-minded in terms of too many different directions being chosen at the same time. Some call this bandwidth or capacity of talent. People who are very talented and driven usually have the capacity to take on tremendous amounts of responsibility and activities that are worthwhile, but that may never be their core passion or purpose. Secondly, double-minded in terms of following popular opinion without forming your own. Double-minded people follow the most popular beliefs, being swayed in their opinions to swing in those directions.

In my own life, I have fallen victim to the bandwidth issue. I have been blessed with the ability to do many things, not everything, but many things. I can lead people, and I am honored to do so; I can analyze data and generate a report; I can take on projects and enlist support to complete the project; I love to play golf and participate in outdoor sports; I can run a business, manage a branch, lead an executive team, preach, teach, coach, and so on. While I don't have any ability in mechanics or construction, I know people who do and enlist their support if the project calls for those skills. While you may be reading this paragraph and saying to yourself "Wow," please don't be impressed. The problem with being able to do so much and loving every part of it is that we can get addicted to the adrenaline rush of doing and miss the one thing we are supposed to be accomplishing. I'm not talking here about working hard or doing what it takes to get a job done. I'm talking about doing so many different things at the same time that you miss the true calling and purpose for your life. Vision can't develop because you are so active doing so many things that none of them becomes the one thing.

At one time in my life, I can remember having a young family, working as a manager at a major commercial bank leading two branches, going to college full-time, serving on two boards in the community, and leading ten different ministry leaders at our small local church. As if that weren't enough, because we needed some extra money at the time, I took on the responsibility of contracting with a major fast food chain to pre-interview potential managers for its expanding market.

Let me just say from experience, this is too much! Some might ask here, "Were you successful?" Well, I was recognized for doing a good job. The problem is that I was so busy doing so many different things that it took me years to realize where I was truly supposed to be. Along the way, I have met people who have so many things going from hobbies to projects that nothing is the most important. We do so many different things in a mediocre way that no one thing is done with excellence. One gentleman I met has a different hobby for each season: hiking in spring, boating and fishing in summer, crabbing in fall, and snowboarding in winter. Alone, this is no problem, but couple this with his running two small businesses, having a full-time job, a growing family, and several new ideas that consume his focus and you can see his ability to do anything with excellence is compromised.

Let's be clear here. We are talking about overcoming vision blockers and shattering barriers to your destiny. I am speaking to those who know there is more to life than just putting in eight hours a day and living someone else's dream. You might read the scenarios above and say there is nothing wrong with what has been described. The issue is that vision is jealous. Your purpose requires your focus and undivided attention. In order to achieve the level of success you know you want, you can't go ten different directions at the same time and take on every project that comes across your path. For those who are happy living at that level, fantastic! Double-minded men and women who focus on the changing winds never reach the fullness of their potential.

How many different activities are you involved in? Take a moment and list them so you have a clear idea of what may be keeping you from moving forward. (If you need additional room, take out a sheet of notebook paper and continue.)

_____   _____
_____   _____
_____   _____
_____   _____
_____   _____
_____   _____
_____   _____
_____   _____

Doing so many things at the same time causes you to become distracted and unfocused. Not the greatest environment for gaining clarity.

MANAGING DISTRACTIONS

How many things are you focused on at the same time? How much time do you dedicate to the most important functions of your personal and professional life? Are you worried about everything but the main thing? So often, there are so many tasks to do, so many important activities needing to be accomplished, and so many projects to complete that none of them get our undivided attention. You can find yourself worried about everything and focused on nothing. I am reminded of a biblical story about Jesus that makes this point perfectly.

Now it happened as they went that He entered a certain village; and a certain woman named Martha welcomed Him into her house. And she had a sister called Mary, who also sat at Jesus' feet and heard His word. But Martha was distracted with much serving, and she approached Him and said, "Lord, do You not care that my sister has left me to serve alone? Therefore tell her to help me." And Jesus answered and said to her, "Martha, Martha, you are worried and troubled about many things. But one thing is needed, and Mary has chosen that good part, which will not be taken away from her." (Luke 10:38-42)

In this story, Jesus had been invited to Martha's house for a visit. He was about to teach some very important kingdom lessons and convey deep spiritual truths that would affect the lives of so many. Martha and her sister Mary were the hosts, but Mary chose to sit and listen to the teaching while her sister Martha was worried about everything in the house being in the right order as well as serving all the guests. To expound, Martha was worried about the place settings, the dinner that would be served, the cleanliness of the home, the amount of seating available, and the interaction of the guests to ensure everyone was mingling. Martha was consumed with worry about all of the activities, so much so that she was missing the most important activity—taking part in this monumental moment in time. Martha complained to Jesus and said, "Don't you care that Mary is not helping me?" Jesus responded with a truth that is directed at more than just Martha. He said, "Martha, Mary has chosen the good part (to focus on the main thing) and that will not be taken from her."

If you learn to focus on the main thing, you can manage the distractions in your life. If you are anything like me, you are constantly being asked to participate in events, activities, movements, conferences, social groups, and the like. Additionally, you are bombarded by 1,000 friends on Facebook communicating everything from their latest family photo to the newest dish they have masterfully prepared. You are connecting on LinkedIn with business people around the world, and being taunted by the endless amounts of information at your fingertips on the Internet. There are family functions, parties, social functions and dinners, coffees and meetings. As if that weren't enough to keep you busy, you are taking on additional projects and trying to find out what you are supposed to do in life. You get involved in community organizations, teach Sunday school, assist in your church, and try to help as many people as you can.

The problem here is that most of us have a Martha complex. Martha was worried about everything but the right thing. So are we! It's time to slow down and take control of the distractions that are keeping us from being single-minded. We need to slow down this very fast-paced world full of distractions and focus on the real purpose of our life. Once we have done that, then it will be time to do everything in our power to make that vision a reality. But to sacrifice the great for the good is not productive or satisfying. It will not allow you to live the life you were meant to live or reap the reward of focusing in one direction.

So often, the lack of our own direction causes us to go in many directions, trying to accomplish many things at the same time. But the power of focus is tremendous! It is time for you to learn the greatest word in the English language and the most difficult one to speak. That word is NO! I realize that society tells us that doing more is how you gain recognition and accolades—doing more is the key to success. I would counter that doing more of the one thing you are called to do is where success lives. Doing more of everything is causing you to be double-minded and lose focus on the most important things in your life. Today is your day to begin telling some of the requests that come your way, "NO!"

Let me give you some keys to managing distractions. Honestly, managing distractions will take some discipline and firm adherence to these principles. Value must be placed on doing the one thing you want to do instead of meeting the demands of everyone else.

1. **Strict Time Management:** One area of my life where I am probably most fanatical besides my faith is time and calendar management. Scheduling time for the things that are most important and managing your life by a strict calendar allows you to say "No" more easily to projects and tasks that are not in line with your goals. Several time management systems are available that work great. I happen to use Outlook by Microsoft and have my calendar synced across all my devices. Get in the habit of scheduling everything and taking time to do so. I spend about fifteen minutes every morning thinking about the day's activities, looking over my appointments, and scheduling things that must get accomplished. This process allows me time to think about what I want to do, what I must do, and what I will allow others to ask me to do. It only works if you are strict about looking at your calendar and recording items as they arise and not accepting them if they conflict with your goals and desires.

2. **Be List-Oriented:** A few years ago, I took a great class from the Franklin Covey Company on time management and acquired some skill in list- and task-oriented management. Participants were instructed to make a list in the early morning of everything that needed to be accomplished and then rank those things in order of importance. You were to place an A by items that must get done today, B by things that should get done today, but could be postponed until tomorrow, and a C by items that can be postponed to a later date. I have adopted this system into my life and found that only on rare occasions do I find myself doing things that are not germane to my goals. Lists keep us focused and allow us to feel accomplished as we complete each

item. They also allow you to see quickly how many different activities you are agreeing to because they must get noted on the list to gain dedicated time.

3. **Use the "Do Not Disturb" Function on Your Phone:** One of the greatest features added to the iPhone was the "do not disturb" function. I have to admit I may use this function a bit too often. The feature allows you to control when email, texts, and calls come through on your phone, thereby only allowing incoming communication from those on your favorites list. While there may be a concern about emergencies, the feature is programmed to allow a call if the number is dialed three times consecutively. Enabling this feature on your phone allows you to be in total control of your time and gives you moments that are free from the bombarding messages and notifications that come in on an hourly basis. Setting up electronic downtime gives you the freedom to think, create, and act on the most important tasks of the day.

4. **Schedule Email, Facebook, and Electronics Time:** This key is difficult in today's world. With the advent of the electronic communication age, individuals are finding that they can accomplish more and more every day. The problem is that it is difficult to prove we are actually more productive. Simply being away from the office for a week's vacation can cause a back log of email three or four hundred deep. Every day, you are tempted to return emails immediately, respond to the cute quip of the Facebook post of your closest friends and family, and reply to the text that came through only moments ago. In fact, millions of dollars are being spent on advertising to keep you from texting and driving, indicating that we are so compelled to see who said what and to respond that we are not focusing on the most important and vital tasks. Don't give in to the immediate need and urge to respond. Schedule time to

return email, post on Facebook or other social media sites, and respond to the electronic draw. Research of the top executives and CEOs reports that each one maintains a high level of discipline regarding how he or she tackles electronic communications. Jeff Weiner, the CEO of LinkedIn, says that he manages his email by tackling it an hour each morning and then cleans it up during whatever show he is watching in the evening. The point is: Don't be compelled to let your electronics manage you.

5. **Plan Your Projects:** As a leader and visionary, you are going to be drawn to many projects and activities. In fact, if you are like me, because you can get things done, many people will ask you to do many others. A key strategy is to know what projects get you to the goal or create the kind of connections you want to make, and then to say "No" to the others. As a leader in a bank, I am asked constantly to support organizations, take part in fundraisers, speak at economic meetings, lead task forces and committees, and give opinions about the goings on in the community. The most important activity I can do is understand which projects I choose to support and say a very kind "NO" to the others.

6. **Write an Annual Personal Business Plan:** Each year around October or November, I take the time to look out over the next year and decide where I want to be and what I want to accomplish. I know there are several major conferences I want to attend and a few major projects I want to complete. In the business community, there are a few tasks I believe I must complete. So I begin to write it all down so I know what I choose to support as I go into the next year. Business leaders write business plans for the future of their companies—the successful business leaders anyway. Why not write a personal plan that details exactly what you want to do next year. Then the only question remaining is how you will execute it.

7. **Schedule Down Time:** I can remember n ~~~~~ business class, taught by the CFO of a m. Portland, Oregon. This class was my first int, world of business and the opportunities that professor taught so many real life and practical concepts that I have carried over into many aspects of my life. One principle he gave was to spend downtime thinking about the future. I have expanded on that principle a bit and actually scheduled downtime. Life gets so busy that the demands can overwhelm even the greatest time manager, but scheduling time where there is no phone, no email, no questions, no demands, no TV, really nothing but you and your thoughts, can be the most productive time. Howard Schultz, CEO of Starbucks, discusses in his book *Onward* how he would frequently visit the very first Starbucks store in Pike's Place in Seattle early in the morning before the store opened. He would spend hours thinking about the company's direction, his leadership of the company, and how to bring value to the shareholders and customers at the same time. He describes this time as some of the most valuable for building his business. He formed plans and opinions during this time while gaining the conviction to execute on those plans. The same has been true for me. I often will schedule time away from everything and everyone just to get alone with my thoughts. Planning for the future and allowing my mind to think and my heart to dream allows me to form very clear pictures of where to go and what to do.

Managing distractions is fundamentally about getting you to the place where you can focus on the most important activities in your life. Double-minded people focus on everything while single-minded people focus on the main thing.

Let's return now to the list of all the activities you wrote down earlier in this chapter. Go through that list and write next to each activity how much time you spend each week on each activity, whether it's five minutes or forty hours. If it's a monthly activity, break it down to a weekly amount of time, so if it's one hour a month, list it as fifteen minutes for the week. Then total all that time to see how many hours a week are consumed with activities. Now go through and determine which activities you can eliminate because they have become vision blockers. I challenge you to trim off five hours a week by eliminating activities that are causing you to be double-minded. Then write down below how you can use that extra time you've created to focus on the one thing that is most important to you:

QUIETING THE MIND

Are your thoughts running away with your vision? One of the fiercest battles fought can be the battle to control your mind. In terms of being double-minded, the thoughts that run through your mind can be overwhelming, distracting, and misleading. Each day you give your mind permission to have the thoughts you have. In order to bring about singularity of mind, you have to take those thoughts hostage. 2 Corinthians 10:5 says, "and we take captive every thought to make it obedient to Christ." Taking thoughts captive and choosing what you will and will not think about gives you power to direct your thoughts to your vision and destiny. The mind is the connector between the spirit and the soul. When there is idle chatter or fast-paced thinking, the messages that should be communicated regarding your vision and destiny can get lost in the fray.

Your mind needs to focus on today and be at peace in that moment. Eighty percent of our thinking is typically about future or past events, and rarely is our mind in the moment. Thoughts are raging and the fast-paced society we live in puts our minds in overdrive, constantly revving our engines until the peace that passes our understanding is lost. When you can slow down your mind and make it quiet with no voices, no chatter, and no chaos, the most profound ideas can begin to materialize. You have mounds of creativity inside of you, dreams waiting to be explored, people waiting to be impacted, and success waiting to be gained. None of that can be realized with a loud mind.

The following four techniques will help you gain control of your thoughts and focus them on your real passion, your true vision.

1. **Find a quiet time and place:** There is a story about two men, Philip and Nathanael, who encountered Jesus in Galilee. Philip was in the city where he met Jesus face-to-face. He was so overwhelmed by this experience that he went and found his friend Nathanael, who was sitting under the fig tree. At Philip's urging, Nathanael went to meet Jesus and Jesus told him about his whole life, including answering questions that Nathanael had been pondering. When Nathanael asked Jesus, "How do you know me?" Jesus replied, "When you were under the fig tree, I met you." Nathanael used this fig tree as a quiet place to sit and meditate, away from the hot sun and many distractions. He would think about the law, his spirituality, various aspects of his life, and contemplate his very existence. Out of that quiet time came a profound experience and revelation from Jesus that gave meaning to all he pondered. I encourage you to have a similar experience by finding a quiet place and a quiet

time where you can be free from distractions—cell phones, email, electronics, family requests, and the like. In my life, I have found that early morning—with a fresh cup of coffee, my Bible, and a window that looks out at the forest—makes the perfect fig tree experience. To quiet your mind, you have to be committed to finding a time and place that allows your mind to slow down and is conducive to your schedule.

2. **Become aware of your thoughts:** As I stated in the opening of this section, 2 Corinthians says we must take captive every thought. To accomplish that task, we have to know what thoughts we're having and evaluate them as ones to keep or ones to disregard. It is amazing to me when I'm "under my fig tree," allowing my mind to go quiet, how bombarded with thoughts I become. Good ones, bad ones, unnecessary ones, unconscious ones—it's at that moment that I gain control over my own mind and don't allow those thoughts to roam freely. Begin to take note of the kinds of thoughts you are having and evict them from your mind. Here is the kind of discussion I literally have with myself: "Eric, I reject that thought and demand that you remain quiet in your thinking." Sounds a bit foolish, but at some point, we have to lead our minds and be responsible for what they are allowed to think.

3. **Focus on your breathing:** Amazingly enough, loud minds make for rapid breathing and rapid breathing makes for fast-paced thinking. If you are trying to quiet your mind, be mindful of your breathing. Slower, longer breaths begin to downshift your mind so you can make room for some of the most profound and creative thoughts you have ever experienced. I know that living in you is one of the most dynamic and prolific world changers that society has ever seen. Get your mind to the place where you are allowed to experience your true vision.

4. **Ask God to give you the mind of Christ:** While I understand this may not ring true to everyone reading this book, in my life, I realize that my mind may not contain the deepest and most profound thoughts. Sometimes, my thoughts wander shallow and aimless without being very productive. 2 Corinthians 2:16 tells us that only Christ knows the inner workings of God and His spirit, so by asking Him to give us the mind of Christ, we can tap into the creativity only He possesses.

Think about your life and its routine. Where might be a good place to call your quiet space?

_____

_____

What time of day would be the best for you to spend quiet time?

_____

Think about the last time you tried to quiet your thinking. Describe what was going on in your mind during those sessions.

_____

_____

Take a moment right now to try and quiet your mind. Focus your thinking and eliminate thoughts that are erroneous or distracting. What things come to your mind?

_____

_____

(Remember the idea is to become aware of your thoughts.)

If you believe in Christ and want to think like him to unlock your creative potential, here is a prayer I've written and regularly recite that may help you:

> God, I know you have created me and fashioned me after your likeness. I realize you have given me my own free will and have put me in this world to make a difference. I also realize that I need the mind of Christ to unlock the creative potential you have for my life. God, I pray that you will give me that mind as I move forward in everything I do. Teach me to possess creativity and world-changing thoughts. Give me ideas that will radically change our world.

BECOMING SINGLE-MINDED

The definition of single-minded is having or showing a single aim or purpose; to be dedicated, resolute, and steadfast; to have one overriding purpose or goal. It is the antithesis of being double-minded. What are you focused on? What is your heart telling you? As you begin to eliminate the distractions and quiet your mind, you will begin to know your core fundamental purpose. The Apostle Paul says, "I do not count myself to have apprehended; but one thing I do, forgetting those things which are behind and reaching forward to those things which are ahead, I press toward the goal for the prize of the upward call of God in Christ Jesus." In other words, I haven't arrived quite yet. I am still searching for the one thing—the one purpose that lies ahead.

The same is true for you. It is time to forget the things that are behind you: the chaos, the contention, the varying opinions, the many, many distractions. Forget them and begin to look forward to the one thing!

Throughout the entire business community are examples of successful people who have had one thing in mind: Let's take Steve

Jobs; he created Apple on one premise: technology that is simple to use. Simplicity has been the cornerstone of the company from its inception. Throughout Apple's existence, the company would scrap any idea that seemed overly complicated or did not provide simple technology for the end user. How about Bill Gates and Microsoft? Bill's vision was to put a PC in every household—to make software a utopian tool and provide access to everyone. Howard Schultz at Starbucks wanted to create a third space atmosphere where Italian style café coffee was served everywhere in the world. In fact, Mr. Schultz describes in his book *Onward* his stern objection to serving food in the stores because it took away from the coffee aroma he sought. Many of the top CEOs and business leaders have that one thing they have to obtain that becomes their sole focus. What is that one thing for you? That is what you must define. Quiet all the other voices and listen for the one thing that speaks to your heart like nothing else does.

Once you can identify that one thing, you will fight for it, finance it, communicate it, and die for it. It becomes the thing that defines you. Being single-minded means being dedicated, resolute, and steadfast. In other words, once you see it and have eliminated your vision blockers, it comes into focus and you will never let it go.

Are you beginning to see? You have eliminated things that caused you to miss the mark, you have conquered strife, and now you are single-minded. What is beginning to come into focus for you? Can you describe that one passion that is burning inside you?

Take a minute and write it down—even if you can't describe it as clearly as you would like. What are you thinking?

_____

_____

_____

STANDING FOR SOMETHING

Earlier, I mentioned that sometimes being double-minded means that you follow the wind of popular opinion. One cliché says, "If you don't stand for something, you will fall for anything." This situation is definitely part of the vision blockers. Personal convictions are powerful motivators to drive a person to reach his or her goals.

I had a friend who would really believe anything someone would tell him. If he were in a crowd of people debating over a political, social, or spiritual issue, he would support whichever side made the most compelling case with the most passionate argument. It was really difficult to have this person as a close friend because you couldn't count on him to counsel or console you when difficulty struck. If you tried to confide in him, it was difficult to tell whether he was giving you sound advice or simply the most convenient advice for that moment based on current circumstances.

I learned from that relationship that if you don't stand for something and there is no solid conviction in you, then you can't possibly help change the world. It became evident to me that a lack of conviction will spill over into all parts of life, making it very difficult to fight for a dream or vision. When it comes to life and reaching your dream, you must take a stand and be firm. No vision comes without controversy. There will always be individuals who will oppose your dream. Without having steadfast faith and personal conviction, how will you maintain the strength to fight under those conditions? Naysayers will always exist, sometimes even among your family members. Lack of conviction will keep you from fighting for what you believe when others oppose or deride your beliefs or goals.

People and brands that stand for something build trust, gain respect, and garner results. History books are full of stories about people who stood for something, and in the process, garnered the world's respect. People from Malcolm X to Gandhi exhibit that having conviction creates respect from others and builds the kind of fortitude that wins!

How do you know what to stand for? In my life, I operate by a set of personal core values. I live my life by these values and look to them for guidance when I am faced with a controversial decision. My core values are:

- God: Living for God always in every way
- Family: Being a faithful, loving husband and supportive father
- Work: Being dedicated to those who hire me and performing above expectations
- Honesty: Always being truthful and honest in all dealings business and personal
- Integrity: To be the same in private as in public
- People: People are more important than any project
- Spiritual Discipline: To live like Christ and to love like Christ
- Unconditional Love: Love people where they are and help them where you can
- Generosity: Live to give and love to give
- Personal Excellence: Excellence inspires others and glorifies God

A great place to start learning to stand for something is to write down your own personal core values:

_____   _____

_____   _____

_____   _____

_____   _____

_____   _____

SUMMARY

Unifying the mind and narrowing its focus is vital to removing double-mindedness as a vision blocker. Too many things going in too many directions at the same time are consuming all of your energy and keeping you from your true calling and living your destiny. It is admirable to try and do everything every time someone calls, but the truth is that each time you take on a project outside your core passion and not in line with your vision, you are delaying your future.

It is time to change your habits and manage all of the distractions, quiet your mind so you can spend some quality time focused on your vision, become single-minded by finding the one thing you are really supposed to accomplish, and finally, develop a set of core values that will help drive you to the promise and keep you from heading in the wrong direction. You are so gifted and the world is waiting to see what you have to offer. Unify your mind and develop your vision!

CHAPTER 5

Overcoming Fear

"Always do what you are afraid to do."
— Ralph Waldo Emerson

In the last chapter, we discussed the vision blocker of a divided mind and the strength and power that comes from having a singular focus based on quieting the mind and taking captive every thought. We learned that you have the ability to take control of your thought life and take it where you want it to go instead of allowing it to run free. In this chapter, we will discuss the vision blocker of FEAR! Probably one of the most profound blockers of vision, fear has the ability to keep you from doing many of the things necessary to live the kind of life you have only dreamed about. Overcoming fear is not only liberating for your vision, but it can allow you the freedom to experience so many good things in life. Over the next several pages, be ready to confront those things that are keeping you from taking your life to the next level.

PARALYZING EFFECTS OF FEAR

Fear is described as a distressing emotional response to perceived danger or threat. At its core, fear is a trigger meant to protect the body from danger or harm. When you approach a hot fire too closely, fear of being burned should trigger a response to move away. When there is an intruder in your home, fear should trigger you to respond by removing the intruder or removing yourself from the situation. When you approach the edge of a high cliff, fear should trigger you not to stand too close to the edge. All of these are very natural occurrences of fear that are healthy for your continued life and protection. The issue with fear is that it also can have a very unhealthy paralyzing effect that must be overcome for you to realize your vision.

For some, fear goes beyond triggering a safety response right into a response that keeps us from moving at all. Fear becomes an excuse not to go further or raise the bar in life. Fear keeps us from speaking in public, trying new things, or experiencing some of the most awesome activities. Fear comes in all shapes and sizes, such as:

- Fear of flying
- Fear of public speaking
- Fear of failure
- Fear of success
- Fear of being outside
- Fear of being inside
- Fear of the unknown
- Fear of being wrong
- Fear of relationships
- Fear of commitment
- Fear of death
- Fear of leadership
- Fear of _____ (add your own phobia)

In many of these cases, fear is paralyzing. The thought of doing one, two, or all of these things may be far too much for your mind or heart to conquer. Even reading about them may cause sweaty palms, impaired breathing, blurred vision, dry mouth, and a desire to put this book down and walk away. Fear keeps you from experiencing life and challenging new activities that will enrich and empower you to do great things.

Dr. Philip Holder says that in extreme cases "fear can manifest itself physically in a number of ways. It can cause tunnel vision, loss of color perception, distortion of both time and depth perception." I can relate to this description so well. I have an extreme fear of needles and, in particular, blood draws. In fact, I am a terrible patient, and much prayer should be directed to any doctor who has the occasion to be my medical professional. I am not sure where the phobia originated, but I know how I respond every time I have a needed blood draw or physical examination. As the doctor suggests a laboratory visit to obtain a sample of my blood, I begin to shake, my hands become very sweaty, and my mind begins to go down an unhealthy path, ultimately resulting in unconsciousness. The doctors have a term for this condition: vasovagal, or an abnormal physiological response, resulting in a symptomatic decline in heart rate and drop in blood pressure, resulting in lightheadedness or total loss of consciousness. I am telling you I am a terrible patient. Every time I have to get a blood draw, it sends my body into this vasovagal response, rendering me unconscious.

Paralyzing effect of fear! While this may seem like an extreme case, I can tell you that for me it is very real and is also very unacceptable. You will notice that in the definition, it says such behavior is an "abnormal response." Fear of this magnitude, therefore, should not render me unconscious; it would be normal for me still to have the ability to function and move forward. Since it is not normal, I have had to learn to overcome the full effects of this response and take steps to work through it. I was not willing to live with the paralyzing effect of fear, and neither should you be. Any irrational fear MUST be overcome.

What is fear keeping you from doing? As you look at going forward in your career and taking on new challenges, what fears make you want to stay right where you are? How about starting that business you always wanted? Does fear keep you from even writing the business plan? What about asking that person out on a date? Are you single today because you won't take the risk and ask him or her out for coffee? While fear was meant to protect us from danger, it can also keep us from so much good.

What are you afraid of? What are some of the things that are causing you to be paralyzed or in some symbolic way to lose consciousness? Can you be honest right now and write down the one thing or several things you fear?

_____

_____

_____

_____

_____

EVERYONE IS AFRAID

In one way or another, we all experience fear! As we go through life approaching different challenges, it is key to remember that everyone has fear. The difference between people's fears is how they handle fear when it challenges them. Do they handle it by panicking or by being courageous? True courage is feeling fear and doing it anyway!

Let's take a look at some famous people who have worked through fear and overcome its effects to help change the world.

Joel Osteen sells out stadiums and speaks live to over 40,000 people per week at his Lakewood Church in Houston, Texas. Osteen says the week before his first sermon in 1999 marked the worst day of his life. "I was scared to death," he says. At the time, he knew very little about speaking or preparing a message. In fact, he was content to sit behind the video camera during his father's sermons. When his father passed away, Osteen's wife and family encouraged him to take the stage. Osteen did so, but he did not overcome his fear for a long time. Conversations from others didn't help. One day, he overheard two ladies saying, "He's not as good as his father." Despite the criticism, he continued to speak, and today, that courage has led to his changing lives around the world.

African-American Rosa Parks was on a bus on December 1, 1955 in Montgomery, Alabama. Parks decided to defy the bus driver's direction to give up her seat in the colored section to white passengers after the white section was filled. Faced with extreme punishment and possibly even death, Parks decided that December 1st was the day to make a stand for her rights. When Parks refused to move, she took a huge risk. She was breaking the law, defying a white bus driver, and not allowing white passengers to sit. All of this to make a statement that has lived on as one of the most historical moments in the twentieth century. Can you imagine the fear she must have felt, and the extreme courage she exhibited in making a stand that day? Her courage helped to fuel the civil rights movement, and today, the U.S. Congress calls her "the first lady of civil rights."

How about a biblical example? As a young man, King David was charged with watching his father's flock and tending to the sheep in the field. King Saul was in power, and the armies of Israel were facing a threat from the Philistine army. The champion fighter, Goliath, stood six cubits and a span (about 9' 6"), and he yelled threats and taunts at King Saul's army, sending fear throughout its ranks. Young David was asked to bring some supplies to his older brothers on the front line. Packing up some cheese and loaves of bread, David began to head toward the battlefield, expecting to see a massive confrontation between the army of Israel and the Philistines. Much to his surprise, David found the troops frightened and the king and commanders huddled in a tent trying to devise a plan. David was amazed that not one soldier would confront the Philistine, leaving him to hurl insults at the army. David told King Saul that he would fight the giant and win victory for the Israelite army. David then approached the giant with a sling and five stones. I am confident that fear was causing his heart to pump more volumes of blood through his veins; his palms must have been sweating, and yet he was confident that he was doing the right thing. The end of the story tells us that David defeated the giant with one stone, and once Goliath had fallen over, David cut off Goliath's head with Goliath's own sword.

Imagine how each of these stories would have been different if the person featured in each one had not pushed through fear to accomplish his or her goal. We know that Joel Osteen is pastor of one of the largest churches in America and is reaching people around the world. We know that Rosa Parks' actions were monumental in the proliferation of the civil rights movement. We also know that David's actions changed the tenor of the war against the Philistines, rewarding the Israelites with freedom and setting the stage for David's eventual reign as king.

What has fear kept you from doing? Think for a moment about your life and describe something you never completed because fear or anxiety caused you to stop or never to start.

_____

_____

_____

_____

How would that story be different if you had pushed through and actually started or completed your dream? Write it down:

_____

_____

_____

_____

OVERCOMING FEAR—A FOUR-STEP PROCESS

Clearly, fear should not control a vision-filled, impassioned, goal-oriented person. We know everyone fears something, and that fear's effects can be paralyzing, so how do we overcome fear? What process should we take to rid ourselves of the debilitating effects of allowing fear to control us?

In 2 Timothy 1:7, Paul writes, "For God has not given us a spirit of fear, but of power, love, and of sound mind." Paul wrote this passage to Timothy when Timothy had accepted his ordination as pastor of a growing church in a city where opposition to the gospel was growing fierce. Timothy had been Paul's student, and now he had been asked to continue his ministry in Ephesus, even though Paul was imprisoned in Rome. Timothy's fear began to grow; he was intimidated at the growing number of opponents, and as a young minister, he was unfamiliar with how to navigate these very troubled waters. Paul sent this message to Timothy to remind him that God had not given him "a spirit of fear" that would keep him from the destiny he was called to achieve.

You can overcome fear through a simple four-step process:

Step One: Recognize What Fear Is. An old cliché I really like that is fitting for this step is the acronym that says F.E.A.R is "False Evidence Appearing Real." Fear is not who you are or how you were made. It isn't reality. Reality is that you are dynamic, powerful, creative, trustworthy, fierce, and able to accomplish phenomenal results in your work, business, non-profit, humanitarian effort, or whatever it is you choose to accomplish. Fear is not how you were created or what you are now. God hasn't given fear to you; therefore, it comes from somewhere else and is used to stop your vision.

Step Two: Embrace the Spirit of Power. 2 Timothy says that you weren't given a spirit of fear; you were given a "spirit of power," a Greek term meaning miraculous power, ability, abundance, and strength violently performing mighty works. This is truly what lives inside of you. A spirit of Power that has the ability to conquer, the ability to rule, the ability to gain abundance, the ability to perform mighty works. It is incredible what can be done by human beings all around the world who embrace the spirit of power. I am sure you have heard many stories of frail people lifting cars to save loved ones who are pinned beneath or entering flame-engulfed buildings to rescue infants trapped in a fire. These stories are all over the media and give us evidence of the kind of power that lives inside each one of us.

Step Three: Use the Spirit of Love to Push Forward. 2 Timothy continues on to say that we were given a spirit of love. It is interesting that Paul uses the term love at this point in his message. The Greek translation of that word is "agape" or "undying, unconditional, intense love." It's the kind of love that says, "I am not going to stop here; I am not going to leave anyone behind, and I will conquer to bring benefit to humanity." This kind of love has a broken heart for the human condition and the condition of our current society. It is the kind of love that is compelled to do something regardless of the cost. This spirit of love pushes you beyond your own fear to action that will change your behaviors forever. Fear plays on selfishness and makes excuses not to take action in an effort to achieve self-preservation. Use love to compel yourself to take action.

Step Four: Enact the Self-Discipline of a Sound Mind. The third spirit Paul says we were given is a sound mind, which means self-discipline—the power to take control over emotions, timidity, and fear. To quote Nike, "Just Do It." The greatest way to conquer fear is to keep doing what you are afraid of doing. Take control of your fear, give yourself a stern pep talk, and just do it. Let me tell you two stories from my own life to illustrate this point.

While I was in the army, I was stationed in Tong Du Chon, Korea. I was assigned to a rear support specialized repair unit charged with ensuring that all assigned units' equipment was battle-ready. While I was in a relatively intense area near the Demilitarized Zone at the border between North and South Korea, the job afforded me the opportunity to travel Korea and take special assignments for training. One week, I decided to take a rappelling course in Cheju Do Island, off the southern coast of South Korea. The first several days of the course were fine, with no real pressure or stress. We spent the days learning to tie off the ropes, how to work with partners, how to place the fasteners into the mountainside for security, how to hold our hands to start and stop, and how to push off the mountainside to continue our descent. All of these lessons took place from the safety of the ground. On the fourth day, it was time to put our training into action, so the instructors took us to the edge of a cliff approximately 1,000 feet up. Each trainee was required to serve in the guide position, the belay position, and to rappel the mountainside. This was all great until I looked over the cliff and realized nothing was really holding me to that cliff but a rope and a d-ring attached to the mountainside. I was able to serve as guide and belay without much difficulty, but when it came to rappelling down the mountainside, I was frozen. It was as if my body wouldn't respond to the neurological commands I was giving it. My mind said, "Everything is going to be okay," but my body sarcastically replied, "Yeah, right." Then I heard the instructor say, "Specialist Scroggins, just jump; I promise your training will take over and you will be fine." As I looked him in the eye, I realized he had done this thousands of times and had inspected our rigging and our process, so I knew he was right. So I "just jumped." As you probably guessed, everything worked out okay since I lived to write about it. Since then, "Just jump" has become sort of an operating guide for me. You must train, prepare, read, and study, but at the end of the day, you need to "just jump" and let your training take over.

The second story involves writing this book. I knew as I wrote the sermon that resulted in this book that it was something I had to do. Everything in me told me that the insights and blockers I was writing about that day were relevant to people around the world who needed to be exposed to solutions for overcoming their vision blockers. For three years, the idea of writing plagued me like an infection whose only cure is that it developed into a written work. I would share with everyone that I was "going" to write a book. Then I realized that I kept telling everyone I was "going to" instead of "I am." When I finally made the decision to write, fear kept me from moving forward. In most areas of my life, I can take on challenges, projects, speaking engagements, new ministries and leadership assignments without too much angst or anxiety. I feel the normal butterflies as I approach each of these, but writing a book meant exposing to the world some of my innermost thinking, secret philosophies, and thoughts. Dear God, what if people didn't like them? What if no one accepted the premise that vision was being blocked by impurity in the heart? What if this and what if that? It was amazing for me to watch my fear paralyze me and keep me from what I believed to be a destiny moment and the beginning of something marvelous. So I took my own advice. I just jumped and began to work on the rough manuscript that eventually developed into the book you are reading.

Fear keeps us from moving forward in so many ways. We are terrified to ask for that raise, terrified to speak in public, terrified to start that business, terrified to take that new job or ministry. But God didn't create us with a spirit of fear; He created us with a spirit of power, a spirit of love, and a spirit of self-discipline. Let's start today identifying that fear is False Evidence Appearing Real, embracing the power in us, using compelling love, and enacting self-discipline to push beyond the limits fear has created. Just Jump!

Think about the last time you tried to accomplish something new or were approached with a new opportunity. Did this experience elicit fear? Describe what you were feeling or thinking.

_____

_____

_____

What evidence did you have that this situation would not have worked out for your benefit?

_____

_____

Describe the power inside of you that can be put to use to overcome this fear. Take a moment and list the strengths you can draw from.

_____

_____

What do you love so passionately that you are willing to go beyond your fear to accomplish it?

_____

_____

In the fourth step, I described using self-discipline to "just jump." What small thing can you tackle today where you can use the just jump philosophy?

_____

_____

FREEDOM FROM FEAR

Freedom is the power to determine action without restraint. Overcoming fear provides freedom for you by allowing you to determine your action and direction without restraint. Our country was built on the premise that we are free from control, restraint, or tyranny, and we believe as a people that this freedom allows us to conquer opportunities that are not available in other countries. When you are not controlled by fear, you have the opportunity to dream and allow your vision to develop. When the paralyzing effects of fear have been overcome, your vision can become reality. What action will you determine to take with your newfound freedom from fear?

Living a life free from fear permits you to go places and do things that were only farfetched dreams before. Remember that you have been created with a purpose, and it's up to you to determine your future level of success.

Consider the story of Corrie ten Boom, a Dutch Christian. Corrie and her family became very active in the Dutch underground, hiding Jews during the Nazi invasion of the Netherlands. In 1942, a Dutch informant gave up information about the ten Boom family and their practice of hiding Jews and providing a means of escape. Corrie and her family were arrested and ultimately placed in the concentration camp at Ravensbruck. Corrie and her sister Betsie together faced some of the most horrific conditions, abuse, and treatment ever endured by humanity. In her book, *The Hiding Place*, Corrie relates that she often didn't know how they were going to make it through the day, but the Word of God and prayer gave them solace and strength during their captivity. Corrie faced many different extreme challenges during her stay in the camps. She was forced to face her fears and overcome them in order to make it through. After her release from the concentration camp, Corrie wrote her book and was subsequently asked to speak to churches, organizations, and special interest groups to share her story. Until her death in 1983, Corrie traveled the world telling her story, encouraging audiences with her message of hope and inspiration to overcome the challenges and obstacles standing in their way. Because of her willingness to overcome her fear, Corrie ten Boom became an inspiration to thousands of people throughout the world. She is noted for saying, "Worry does not empty tomorrow of its sorrow; it empties today of its strength."

Obviously, Corrie ten Boom faced unfathomable circumstances. Fear must have gripped every person who entered that concentration camp. Most likely your situation is not as dramatic or as dire, yet when you face your fears, your feelings can be just as intense.

Corrie was able to encourage an entire generation by overcoming her fear. What could you accomplish by overcoming yours?

Take a moment and think about overcoming your fear and experiencing freedom from that fear. What would you accomplish? Describe in detail what you think your accomplishment might be.

_____

_____

_____

_____

SUMMARY

Fear is paralyzing and debilitating, keeping us from taking risks, conquering challenges, or otherwise moving forward. It can and will keep you from doing what is necessary to achieve your goals and realize your destiny. The process is very clear—we have been given the spirit of power, the spirit of love, and the spirit of self-discipline or sound mind to move us beyond fear to a place of effectiveness. It is up to you to embrace these things. Take the risk and just do it.

As with my rappelling experience, the time has come for you to "just jump." Take a leap of faith; realize that you are better than you think you are and your gifting will take over. There are so many wonderful things waiting for you once you conquer fear. Realize that fear is simply False Evidence Appearing Real and move into your future with power. You can have the same world-changing effect as Corrie ten Boom after the concentration camp, King David after Goliath, or any number of other people who have pushed beyond the fear.

Just Jump!

CHAPTER 6

Identifying the Pharisee

"Often, the less there is to justify a traditional custom,
the harder it is to get rid of it."
— Mark Twain

Over the past several chapters, you have discovered several tools to overcome several vision blockers in your own life. You learned how to make the right decisions and choices to hit your mark, how to uncover the evil beneath the surface called strife, how to focus your mind to avoid being double-minded, and how to address the paralyzing effects of fear. Each one of these vision blockers has the ability to keep you from seeing where your true calling and destiny lies. In this chapter, we are going to talk about a vision blocker so subtle that you may not even realize it's at work in your life—it is that effective.

I have termed this phenomenon the "Pharisee Complex." What exactly is a Pharisee Complex? In the gospels, Jesus addresses the Pharisees on multiple occasions. The Pharisees were a Jewish religious sect in Jesus' time. They spent years studying the laws of God and interpreting them for the people. Their roles were much like those of pastors or rabbis today, only they were totally focused on the fulfillment of the Law, and in some cases, they made the Law fit their needs instead of having their lives fit the Law. They were continually in conflict with another religious sect of the time, the Sadducees, over social, political, and religious issues, which would cause major rifts between the two groups. To say that the Pharisees were controlled by a spirit of religion would be an understatement; they were known to be the most studious of the Law, yet the most ignorant of its true purpose and design.

The Pharisees were the group that should have been most aware and understanding of Jesus' ministry, yet they completely misunderstood his purpose and calling. They did not see him as the Christ. Totally blinded by their traditionalism, legalism, and religion, they missed the most profound event in history. Is traditionalism, legalism (strict adherence to a system), and religion keeping you from seeing the great purpose for your life?

BLINDING EFFECTS OF A PHARISEE

How is this Pharisee Complex keeping you from seeing your destiny? The effects of strong traditionalism can keep us from having the freedom to move forward. It can be so amazing and saddening to watch very talented people not reach their highest potential all because they're locked in an old tradition or system (family, culture, class, or otherwise). We are blind to the possibilities afforded us when we can only see as far as the "way it's always been done." Here is one example from the Bible of how blinding this situation can be:

> Now it happened on another Sabbath, also, that He entered the synagogue and taught. And a man was there whose right hand was withered. So the scribes and Pharisees watched Him

closely, whether He would heal on the Sabbath, that they might find an accusation against Him. But He knew their thoughts, and said to the man who had the withered hand, "Arise and stand here." And he arose and stood. Then Jesus said to them, "I will ask you one thing: Is it lawful on the Sabbath to do good or to do evil, to save life or to destroy?" And when He had looked around at them all, He said to the man, "Stretch out your hand." And he did so, and his hand was restored as whole as the other. But they were filled with rage, and discussed with one another what they might do to Jesus. (Luke 6:6-11)

This event was the third Sabbath in a row when Jesus had gathered large groups of people. On the first, he honored tradition by doing no work on the Sabbath. On the second, he and his disciples were hungry, so as they were walking through the grain fields, they plucked a few heads of grain, rubbed them in their hands, and ate them. On this third one, Jesus healed a man suffering from a crippled right hand. Jesus' true mission was one of freedom, liberation, salvation, and fulfillment of the Law. In Matthew 5:17, Jesus tells us, "Do not think that I came to destroy the Law or the Prophets. I did not come to destroy but to fulfill." He was the Savior promised to the world. History was waiting for this moment, the moment a savior was born who would eventually be crucified for the redemption of sin. The issue here is that while the Pharisees believed in strict adherence to the Law, they couldn't see that the person the Law was waiting for was standing right in front of them. Their tradition, legalism, and strict adherence to their system of worship and religious living was standing in the way of their vision.

I believe the same things happens to us. We get so caught up in our traditions, family systems, culture, habits, and so on that we can't see our own futures. Traditionalism blinds us and keeps us from seeing different ways of thinking and acting that would present opportunities to us. We turn off and tune out when someone challenges us to think differently, and we are constantly assessing the new against the old and justifying the old. Traditional thinking has at its core the tenet that things should always be as they have been and no other way. This type of thinking celebrates the status quo and victimizes those who challenge it. You are martyred for having critical, creative, or original thinking.

Think about this situation in terms of culture. Maybe you are part of a very strong culture that has overwhelming expectations that you act a certain way, think a certain way, or live a certain way. This strong influence in your life can keep you from taking on new challenges or doing things a bit differently. While your cultural heritage can definitely make you a stronger, more grounded person, deep traditional thinking can surely block your vision. Like the Pharisees, you can become so steeped in tradition that the vision in front of you is out of sight.

Breaking down this traditionalism, legalism, and strict religious adherence will liberate your vision and cause you to see things in a whole new way.

Can you think of some traditional thought processes or systems at work in your life? Take a minute to list them below and evaluate the way you think. Is it critical thinking or traditional thinking? Do you have original ideas, or are your ideas ones that were passed down from generation to generation?

_____   _____

_____   _____

_____   _____

_____   _____

QUESTIONING TRADITIONAL THINKING

It's time to break the mold and begin to do things differently. Traditional thinking, also known as popular thinking, is widely accepted and keeps everyone who subscribes to it in a stasis of sorts. The boat isn't rocked, there are no waves, and you are mindlessly placed in this path of popular thinking that keeps you going where everyone else is going without challenging whether that direction is right for you. Breaking traditionalism or questioning popular thinking is quite unpopular and yet so powerful.

Today, we no longer live in the dark. Each of our homes, offices, shopping centers, streets, and parking lots has lights that shine bright, creating the ability for us to see in the dark. I am confident that anyone who has experienced a lightbulb fully appreciates its application and function in our day-to-day lives. Had Thomas Edison stuck to the tradition of lighting an oil lamp or been satisfied with the world remaining dark after sunset, we would not have the lightbulb today. Instead, even as a young boy, Edison was always researching and studying to find ways to do things differently. When he received a book full of experiments, he tried every one of them. Widely credited with creating the research laboratory, Edison was never satisfied with thinking or doing things like everyone else. He was in a constant pursuit to do things differently so he could find solutions to everyday issues and concerns. He is credited with over 1000 patents for inventions such as improved telegraph devices, the phonograph, the lightbulb, devices for maintaining constant voltage, the motion picture camera, and many others, which became the foundation for many of the household items we use today.

In his book *The Checklist Manifesto*, published in 2009, Atul Gawande talks about the importance of checklists and creating systems that ensure processes and procedures are completed correctly. As a trained surgeon, he noticed the elevated number of patients who were having complications in surgery and in post-surgery recovery. He began to track the number of instruments left in patients that resulted in follow-up surgery and infections; the number of bacterial infections from improper scrubbing in procedures; and the disinfection of the instruments prior to surgery that caused complications for patients. Despite the long history of medicine and surgery, Atul found that no common or consistent method existed for performing the pre-procedure process. He based his thesis on the idea that we are so advanced in our knowledge of what we can do that we fail at the simple tasks leading up to major activities. He contends that the "lowly checklist" is the solution to creating a higher success rate and more effective use of our knowledge and expertise.

Popular thinking would tell us that we have moved beyond the checklist; that this simple tool is ridiculous and unnecessary in our very advanced world. However, Atul Gawande has revolutionized the medical profession, government agencies, and the financial industry by reintroducing us to the checklist.

What is wrong with following the popular or widely accepted way of thinking? Why question traditional thinking? There are several reasons:

1. **Traditional Thinking Requires No Creativity:** Traditional thinking thinks the way everyone else thinks. It sees things the way we have always seen them, and it is not interested in looking for more creative or efficient ways. Group think tells you your opinion, gives you your viewpoint, and tells you your destiny. It requires no creativity because you aren't challenging anything.

   There is a funny story about a lady who made the most amazing roast. She was recognized all over the community for her wonderful roast and the full flavors it offered. She had a very particular way of making the roast. She would add all the seasonings and rubs to prepare the meat for cooking, and just before she placed it in the pan, she would cut both ends off. When asked where she learned to make the roast, she explained that it was a recipe her mother had passed down. She explained that she made the roast exactly the way her mother had made it—seasonings, process, cut ends, and all. The lady was pushed further to find the origin of the recipe and called her mother. Mom explained that she had learned how to make the roast from her mother. She would mix the seasoning, place the rub, prepare the meat, and cut the ends just as her mother did. Everything was the same. The lady asked where her grandmother had learned to prepare the roast. Curiosity was now mounting, so the grandmother was asked where she learned to make the roast. The grandmother said, "I learned from my mother." She explained that she created the same seasonings and rub that she had passed down to her daughter and then down to the granddaughter. But in her explanation, she left out cutting off the ends. Curiously, the grandmother was asked, "Did your mom cut off the ends as well?" The grandmother explained that she had, in fact, started that process. With great anticipation, the grandmother was asked, "Why do you cut off the ends?" She replied, "It's very simple; my roast pan wasn't big enough, so the only way I could make it fit was to cut off the ends."

Traditional thinking requires no creativity. People continue to cut off the ends of the roast without even questioning the reason behind it.

2. **Traditional Thinking Is Mind-Numbing:** Traditional thinking doesn't require you to think for yourself. It is mind-numbing because you are following the trend created by the thinkers rather than thinking for yourself. Following traditional think-

ing puts you in some sort of social comfort zone and allows you to exist without any resistance or conflict. You can put your brain on autopilot and not engage in thoughts that change your circumstances or financial standing. Traditional thinking says, "After college, get a job, work there for thirty years, and then retire." There may be more for you—perhaps you are meant to start a business, create a new product, and invent new equipment. But traditional thinking doesn't allow you to explore any of those possibilities.

3. **Traditional Thinking Keeps You Average:** In his book *The 10X Rule: The Only Difference Between Success and Failure*, Grant Cardone says that "Average is a Failing Formula." The plague of the middle class is average performance—doing enough to meet average activity levels and receive average wages. Coasting into retirement, these people make average decisions to be average like everyone else. Dave Ramsey says, "Live today like no one else so that tomorrow you can live like no one else." Traditional thinking keeps you broke, mediocre, and building someone else's dream. Traditional thinking says that you only invest in a portfolio to build up your assets until you are old enough to take them out in distribution during a time called retirement. It never considers wealth-building strategies or taking a risk by building your business. But what about market conditions, a changing economy, and all the circumstances you can't plan? Traditional thinking says that there will be enough to be average and mediocre.

In a downturn economic environment, companies do the traditional things: they cut costs and consolidate departments. When things get tough economically, companies begin to shut down the creative, hunker down, and control expenses, hopefully cutting enough to keep the doors open and the lights on. They begin to look for average performance from their employees, their senior management teams, and their vendors. Average performance that doesn't rock the boat too much and allows them to eke out a return. This kind of traditional thinking actually puts the company in a stifling mode of mediocrity that can be tough to break. It becomes average. For some, so average that they fail.

Can you identify some people around you who are stuck in traditional thinking?

_____

_____

How many people do you know who can see the potential in their own lives because they do not see things the way everyone else sees them?

_____

_____

EMBRACING CREATIVE THINKING

Creative thinking is the ability to look at problems or situations from a fresh perspective and suggest unorthodox solutions that may look unsettling at first. It requires looking at your life, dream, problems, or situations with a fresh set of eyes—eyes that are not bound by tradition, religion, law, a system, or an organization. It is looking at things through the perspective of possibility rather than probability.

Creative thinking asks, "What are the possibilities in this situation?" Traditional thinking asks, "What is probable in this situation?" Too often, we are limited by what we think is probable instead of what is possible. As a Christian, I often have to look at things in my life and realize there are possibilities outside my control—things that can take place in God's infinite wisdom and power that are typically limited in my own carnal, human state of being. Creative thinking taps that source of creativity and says, "You are not limited" and "Resources are limitless."

Being able to embrace creative thinking takes four critical steps:

1. **Be prepared to be unpopular:** Creative thinkers are typically operating outside of a box. Most of the time, creative thinkers don't even realize there is a box. The solutions derived by creative thinkers are wild and zany, oozing with possibilities not even considered by traditional thinkers. Because creative thinkers aren't looking at tradition, systems, or group think to solve a problem, they are often considered risky or out in left field. But it's this type of thinking that allows you to tap into the kind of creativity that begins to form your vision. The Pharisees could only see Jesus as a good teacher (sometimes not even that) or a renegade leader. Because of their traditionalistic view, they missed the fact that he was compassionate, powerful, and there as a savior. The disciples, on the other hand, were creative thinkers. They embraced the idea that the miracles, the compassion, and the teachings were so profound and outside the box that Jesus had to be something special.

2. **Try Something New:** Creative thinkers are explorers constantly on the lookout for possibility. It isn't uncommon to see a critical thinker taking on new challenges, questioning the norm, or bucking the trend. They are willing to try new things and take some risks. When is the last time you took a risk or tried something new? Traditional thinkers want you to believe that what has always been done is what always needs to be done. Creative thinkers, on the other hand, look for new ways to do things and are exploring new solutions to problems old and new.

   The apostle Peter was a creative thinker. Matthew 14 tells the story of a massive storm that was blowing while he and his partners were in a boat on their way across the lake. The storm began to blow harder and harder and tossed the boat all over the lake. Jesus, seeing the men in distress, decided to walk on the water in an effort to prove his divinity and compassion for his friends in trouble. As he approached the boat, Peter saw Jesus and asked whether he could come out on the water as well. In a shocking response, Jesus said, "Come." Peter got out of the boat and began to walk on water—something no human before or since has accomplished. Peter didn't limit his thinking to what physics, biology, chemistry, or anatomy said was possible. He saw the opportunity to do something way outside of the box and succeeded at walking on water. That is creative thinking and really trying something new.

Your business needs you to try something new. I mentioned earlier that in an economic downturn, companies typically think traditionally. They cut expenses and consolidate departments. What about taking the opportunity to try something new—something more creative? How about having a "water walking" idea that looks at things in a completely different way? Instead of trying to cut expenses, why not grow revenue? Why not keep the creativity in your company and try to add new products, services, or a new line of business that can add additional revenue to the top line and drive additional profit to the bottom line? Bold, I know, but great companies are willing to try something new.

3. **Challenge the Tradition or Popular Belief:** President Abraham Lincoln is a prime example of challenging popular belief systems. His belief in a modernized, slave free, progressive America was met with such fierce opposition that it thrust the country into civil war. Lincoln persisted despite the opposition, constantly challenging the traditional and looking forward to the possibilities of a free, modern America.

Traditional thinking is keeping you locked away from your destiny and locked in mediocrity. Challenge that thinking and realize that what resides in you is creativity, passion, power, and success. You can do things that have never been done in your family history. You can go where no man has gone before. You have the ability to challenge the status quo and do something different. So Do It!

4. **Constantly Evaluate Your Own Thinking:** From time to time, I ask myself a series of questions to assess whether I am thinking the way my family wants me to think or whether I am thinking creatively. So often we can revert back to tradition and begin to make systematic decisions for our life based on our culture or upbringing. To combat this tendency, constantly evaluate your thinking and make sure you are in the creative zone.

I ask:

- Is this thought creative or traditional?
- Where do I believe it originated?
- What is everyone else in this situation doing?
- How is that working for them?
- Why do I think the way I think?
- Do I believe God is inspiring this thought, or did some manmade idea give it to me?

Often, I will engage in a session of unbridled thought and exploration of my mind. I just want to create and begin dreaming about the possibilities that exist. What do I really want to do with my life? Where do I see myself in five years? What passion is driving me today? If I had all the money in the world, what would I do?

It is amazing how a series of questions similar to this can open your mind to think outside the box and allow you to dream and see the vision that is waiting to be birthed inside of you.

IDENTIFYING THE PHARISEE COMPLEX

As I stated earlier, the Pharisees were steeped in tradition, law, and legalism. They could not see beyond the ends of their noses, and they were not willing to accept what they could not explain. Their thinking was traditional and would not even consider the creative. How do you identify the Pharisee Complex in yourself? What are the signs that your vision is being blocked by this very real issue?

By looking at the Pharisees, we can begin to identify the characteristics keeping us blocked and locked. The Pharisee Complex is marked by the following characteristics:

1. **Culture over Future:** A person suffering from the Pharisee Complex is very concerned with keeping his culture in tact at the expense of his future or individual dreams. Culture trumps all.

2. **Finding Yourself Frustrated:** The Pharisee Complex keeps its victim frustrated and on edge. You notice there is something inside of you that wants to break out, but you don't release it because that would be breaking with tradition. This pent up desire and dream begins to frustrate and irritate you.

3. **Opportunity Is Never Knocking:** Because opportunities typically come to those who are on the move and ready to take on the challenge, the Pharisee Complex is void of opportunity. Typically, the thinking is so traditional that opportunity is never considered. "This is the way we have always done it" is the mantra.

4. **Criticizing Others:** The Pharisee Complex is rich in accusation and criticism. A study of the New Testament shows that each

encounter with the Pharisees was a heated one. The Pharisees were quick to try to trip up Jesus. They were always devising plans to prove he wasn't who he said he was.

5. **Change Is Extremely Difficult:** While the Pharisees should have been on the lookout for the Messiah, they were instead on the lookout for those breaking the law. They were consumed by what was, instead of looking at how the times had changed. The Pharisee Complex causes a vehement resistance to change. Those who suffer from it are so enthralled with the religious, the cultural, and the popular pathway that change is never an option for them.

6. **Threatened by Others' Success:** The Pharisee Complex doesn't want anyone to see things differently. It keeps its participants so deeply ingrained in tradition that success is seen as a threat. If you are successful, chances are you have challenged everything that the Pharisees stood for and your success begins to point out their deficiencies.

7. **Dreaming about the Good Ol' Days:** The Pharisee Complex lives more in the past than the present and definitely not in the future. This complex constantly remembers when times were better and things were better. The past is where all the stories come from without any regard for what could happen in the future.

8. **More Interested in Family/Friends' Opinions than Your Own Dream or Vision:** The Pharisee Complex is convinced that the traditional way is the only way, and therefore, its adherents will only listen to those who have the same opinion. Creative thinking will cause too much disruption in the status quo and, therefore, isn't considered.

These characteristics, in part or in total, are present in those suffering from the Pharisee Complex. This tragic complex is violently and vehemently opposed to the vision that takes you to your destiny. Each encounter with the Pharisees was a strong opposition to humanity's future. The Pharisees were called many things from hypocrites to brooding vipers. These labels were harbingers of the tragic end awaiting those who showed allegiance to this way of thinking. It's time to break out of the Pharisee Complex and overcome the Pharisee in You!

Take a few moments to see whether these characteristics are present in you. Answer the following questions honestly so you can begin to see things differently.

1. How often do you write down a vision or dream? Do you spend time promoting your culture or your individual future?

2. Think about recent encounters with others. Do you find yourself easily frustrated or even irritated by others—especially if they begin to talk about plans for their lives?

3. When was the last time you were presented with an opportunity to change what you are doing for a living or to be part of something great? How did you respond?

4. Are you the person in the group who is celebrating others or criticizing them? Do you have a quick wit that you use to cut others down, or are you building them up?

5. Think about your life—are you change-oriented, or do you like things just the way they are? When presented with new roles at work, church, or at home, how do you respond?

6. When others in your life tell you stories of their exploits and successes, how do you respond?

7. Do you have hundreds of stories about the way things used to be and very few, if any, about your dreams and future?

8. Whose opinion is the most important in your life? Do you find any value or place any trust in your own opinion? When you articulate a dream or vision, do you quickly disregard it as silly?

OVERCOMING THE PHARISEE IN YOU

You may have read the previous section and been shocked by what you found. One, maybe all, of the characteristics are present in your life. Up to this point, you haven't given those characteristics much attention other than noting that things were not happening for you, and for some reason, this life of promise turned quickly into a life of frustration and mediocrity. I know and hope you know that isn't your destiny. You have been created with a definite purpose to do great and mighty things in this life. You are here on purpose for a purpose, regardless of your past or the Pharisee living in you. Let's take some steps to rid your life of that Pharisee Complex forever.

In August of 2005, I was asked to become the senior pastor for an ailing church in Tacoma, Washington. It was a great opportunity for a guy who had served most of his ministry time as an associate pastor. I was really eager to take the lead role in my own church pulpit, and the circumstance miraculously worked out so I was able to transfer my residence to Tacoma from Vancouver and continue in my day job as a regional manager for a major bank while I served as pastor for this well-established, but underpopulated church. Truthfully, the church only had fourteen in attendance, including me, my wife, and two kids. Church membership numbers aside, I was eager to start this new chapter and take on a challenge I had yet to tackle. Prior to accepting the role of senior pastor, I spent time developing my skills as a preacher through various opportunities to speak that had been presented. After one of these occasions, a pastor friend, for whom I had great respect, counseled me that my style of preaching wasn't relevant or impactful. He was more of a teacher, and possessed a calm, mellow delivery that was rich in educational format, much like you would see in a college classroom or in a lecture hall. My style was motivational and passionate, and I delivered it with high energy and high impact content. I liked to use humor, stories, and rich historical content that placed the listener into the setting of the story and the message. This pastor had mentioned his dislike of my preaching style on a couple of occasions, which left a lasting impression on me that I probably needed to change my delivery.

Coming to this new church, I was full of excitement and zeal to deliver what was in my heart that filled me with passion. Helping people had always been on the top of my priority list, and now I had the opportunity to do it in a big way, or so I thought.

The first three months I was in this new church, I couldn't understand what was happening. I was frustrated and irritated by the services. Instead of leaving the pulpit with high energy and passion, I was leaving feeling confused and irritated, and I dreaded going back the next week. We added a few people to the congregation, but I could tell the impact of my preaching was not what I was used to or what I had desired. I was trying to deliver my message with the same eloquence as this pastor, using his format of communicating. I was sure that what he had told me was true and that my old style was not appropriate. His voice was in my ear, telling me that his way was the right way, and each week, I became more and more frustrated, trying to execute on his advice.

After about three months, I couldn't take it anymore. I was praying and studying, and my topic for the next Sunday—based on the story of King David in 2 Samuel dancing in the streets when the Ark of the Covenant was brought to Jerusalem—excited me so much that I couldn't contain my enthusiasm. I ran into the kitchen and told my wife, "I can't take it anymore! I can't preach the way he preaches. I can't teach that way; it's like I have fire inside of me and I need to let it out." This realization was the transformation I needed and what the church needed. From that point forward, people were inspired by my message, my passion returned for what we were building, there was freedom in the church, and people were so excited to be part of a great movement that soon more and more people were added to our congregation.

That was the moment I learned that I can't listen to others to determine my future. I had to overcome the Pharisee Complex and live my own vision.

Ironically, the steps to overcome the Pharisee Complex are in direct opposition to the characteristics that keep you there. Let's explore them and put them into action in your own life:

1. **Prefer Future over Culture**: You have a vision inside of you that is valid and powerful. It is the key to your future and your destiny. Make it a priority regardless of cultural, familial, or societal influences. Explore the future and put it first.

2. **Release the Vision:** I was so frustrated trying to live others' expectations for my life, my ministry, and my career. It wasn't until I released the vision inside me that I found freedom to soar.

3. **Create Opportunity:** Someone once told me that it's hard to get to a destination in a car that doesn't move. Be on the move creating opportunity. Do something different today. Don't sit there in your culture, tradition, and stoic life, waiting for something to happen. You make it happen.

4. **Celebrate Others:** Make the decision today that you are going to celebrate others around you. Relationships are the currency of success. They are the most important thing in life—celebrate them. Be on the lookout for what others are doing and celebrate with them.

5. **Embrace Change:** The ancient Greek philosopher Heraclitus once said, "The only thing constant in life is change." Become a change agent. Start to look for things that have been the same for decades and find solutions or a different way of doing what you always do and make the change.

6. **Encourage Others' Success:** You will be surprised by how successful you become when you encourage others to succeed. Be the voice to those around you that tells them, "You can do it," and then you will be shocked by how much you begin to believe "You can do it" as well.

7. **Dream/Dream/Dream:** You can probably remember being a child and dreaming about some grand plan or exotic future you hoped to explore. Somewhere along the way, someone told you that dreams were for kids and unrealistic. Let me tell you that dreams are extremely valuable. Drive around the neighborhood you want to live in, go to a conference and hear a speaker deliver a destiny speech, watch successful people impacting the world, and dream. Get your dream back and don't let it go.

8. **Defend Your Opinion and Celebrate the Difference:** Remember the old cliché "If you don't stand for something, you will fall for anything." It's time to gain some confidence in your position, your opinion, and your dream. Don't be afraid (you already conquered fear) to tell others your story and defend its validity to you.

If you put these eight strategies in place in your life, I believe you will overcome the Vision Blocker of the Pharisee Complex and drive your life to a new level of success.

SUMMARY

Some call it "stinkin' thinkin'." I call it the Pharisee Complex; either way, traditionalism, culture, legalism, or religion is keeping you from seeing what your future can hold. I hope you can see how group think, tradition, or doing things you have always done can limit your calling and vision. You have been created as an original. There is no one else like you. You are amazing, possess such powerful gifts, and have a valid dream. It isn't silly, unrealistic, or childish. Tradition will tell you that it is and that you are never going to be successful unless you stay within the confines of that tradition or model that worked for your father, grandfather, and great-grandfather. The truth is that while they may have been successful in their lives, their dreams are not your dreams.

So break with tradition, break with culture, break with legalism, and find yourself living your own vision and dream.

CHAPTER 7

Healing the Pain of Your Past

"Love bears all things, believes all things, hopes all things, endures all things."

— 1 Corinthians 13:7

Endures all things indeed! Over the past several chapters, we have discussed several vision blockers and how to overcome each one. From failing to hit the mark to the Pharisee Complex, each vision blocker you overcome allows your vision to gain clarity and precision. Removing each of these obstacles allows you to gain perspective on what you have been placed here to accomplish. Each one of these blockers is imperative to remove, but none is so important as the Pain of Your Past.

Each one of us carries a degree of disappointment and discouragement that we must find ways to overcome, but what about the emotional scars from some tragic, deliberate, or calculated action caused by someone or something in your life? Pain in our past is of great consequence to our future. It either fuels our passion to overcome and be tremendously successful, or it chains us to the feelings of despair, depression, lack of self-esteem, hurt, and distress that keep us from moving forward. This particular vision blocker traps you and locks you down. Its pain and hurt lead to anger, frustration, and bitterness, which soon leads to a life that has been spent plotting revenge or retaliation on all those whom you encounter. It's time to overcome the Vision Blocker of Pain from Your Past.

A WOUNDED LIFE

Stories of tragedy never cease to amaze me. People in our society have been through some incredible things, and they are left with lives that are wounded. So many people have endured sexual, physical, and emotional abuse, and other actions that take advantage of another person's personal space and liberty. Each of these forms of abuse causes pain that runs very deep and creates a wounded life wrought with feelings of anger, depression, despair, embarrassment, and shame—all very unproductive emotions that will keep you locked down right where you are.

I understand very clearly how this cycle can manifest in a life. I had a fairly troubled upbringing beginning with my teenage years. My mom was fantastic; she was always very supportive and encouraging. Her hands were very comforting, and she always had an encouraging word to speak after a very crazy day. I can remember the times when my siblings and I were young kids and we would drive from Tennessee to visit our family in Texas for the holidays. My uncles, aunts, and cousins were always such a welcome sight and full of love. We always had a great time singing, talking, and eating great meals made with Mexican flair. Times were great for everyone, including me, until I turned thirteen. I'm not sure what prompted the change, but at that time, my dad took a very wrong turn that devastated my life. I had always thought things were different between him and me; my relationship with him just didn't seem to be the same as my siblings' relationships with him. I couldn't quite put my finger on it, but I knew something was different. Then when I turned thirteen, my father began to take advantage of me in ways that are inappropriate for any father/son relationship. What started as innocent or accidental brushing past me turned into something much worse and far more embarrassing for an awkward thirteen-year-old boy. Over a period of three years, he continued this completely unacceptable behavior. It wasn't until I was sixteen and was able to take some weightlifting classes, tied in with track, cross country, and high school wrestling, that I gained the confidence to stand up to and overcome his constant and incessant touching.

Not the childhood you dream about for sure. An already awkward relationship that just didn't quite make sense had turned into one of sexual abuse, leading to a very frustrated, embarrassed, and confused teenager. This abuse hurt me in places that, until then, I didn't know existed. While my mother was completely innocent and always encouraging me to be the best I could be and to reach for the stars, she had no idea what I was secretly dealing with. At seventeen, I joined the United States Army, sensing I had no other options for college financing, but primarily, to escape the horror of having to look my father in the face every day. This abuse caused so many crazy fears and frustrations. I didn't date anyone until late into high school, and I was afraid of other people, primarily girls. I couldn't speak to others and had a difficult time making friends. My tour in the Army was good for me. Basic and Advanced Individual Training gave me back some self-confidence.

I was beginning to make great progress until I turned twenty-one. That was the year I learned that my father, the man who took advantage of a vulnerable teenage boy, wasn't biologically related to me. I was actually the biological son of a man my mother had met while he was in the Air Force. It was a very emotional and confusing year. I can remember sitting in the living room of my parents' home as my mother and abusive stepfather told me what had happened; I began to feel more and more isolated as I realized the truth. I became angry, frustrated, and even embarrassed because it was as if everyone knew but me. Here I was going through this hell as a teenager, and I was not even his child, and no one could see the signs. I was hurt beyond belief.

To make matters worse, one day I asked my mother to contact my true biological father to let him know I wanted to speak with him. It wasn't long before we were talking on the phone. I was hoping to let him in on a great gift—me. Somehow, I thought that hearing his voice and letting him know I was alive would in some way make him want to see me because he would realize what he was missing. That couldn't have been further from the truth. This man didn't want me when I was born, and he still didn't want me. On the phone, he acted completely uninterested and basically severed any possibility for a relationship.

So there I was, raised by a man who had abused me and disowned by the man who had fathered me. You can probably imagine the feeling of abandonment that plagued my mind, and further, what that could do to a person's self-esteem, psyche, confidence, and life. For a period of my life, all of this pain did exactly what it was intended to do—steal my vision. It caused me some deep emotional pain and completely shattered my confidence. Its design was to leave me without a dream, without a vision, and without hope. Boy, did it lose!

I understand what a wounded life feels like. Even as I write this, I am overwhelmed by compassion for your situation and know that there is healing for the pain in your past. I know you can overcome and that you don't have to live with any of it anymore. I didn't have to live with it and neither do you. Writing this story down has had a somewhat therapeutic effect on me. I encourage you to write yours down as well. What pain have you suffered? The loss of someone important, the inappropriate touch of someone in your life, escaping a physically abusive situation, a major failure such as a marriage, business, or job? Whatever the case, take time here to write it down. We are going to deal with it together.

_____

_____

_____

_____

_____

_____

_____

_____

_____

_____

CARRYING LUGGAGE FULL OF PAIN

I have traveled with many people on mission trips, speaking engagements, and vacations. I always find it interesting to see what people are going to bring with them. My wife and I have some very close friends we travel with on a fairly regular basis, and I am always amazed by how much luggage they need on even the shortest of trips. Saundra and I have narrowed our travel luggage down to a level that makes us flexible and quickly able to adjust our plans. Usually, we take one suitcase and then a carryon bag for a laptop, notepad, and incidentals that may be needed during the mid-travel process. Our friends usually check several bags, plus the carryon and briefcase. So much luggage makes the trip cumbersome and really difficult when needing to adjust to changing plans or opportunities that arise during the trip.

Often, we are carrying the pain of our past with us in life like the luggage my friends carry on their trips. When you are carrying this pain with you, life becomes inflexible, difficult to adjust to, and opportunities are missed. This pain-filled luggage has become so familiar to you that you wouldn't know how to exist without it. You have all sorts of designer luggage labeled with different types of pain. You never leave home without it.

As our friends experience on their trips, that luggage becomes very heavy; carrying it around makes your life very difficult and labor intensive. My friends carry all that luggage with them because they are trying to be prepared for any circumstance that may arise. They have contingency plans in their luggage that will hopefully address any situation that arises. Some call it prepared—I call it paranoid. Instead of being confident in their plans and definitive in which engagements they will accept, they try to prepare for all of them. Saundra and I realize we may not be prepared for some events not included in the original itinerary so we may have to take a quick trip to the store or choose not to attend an event, but that is a small inconvenience compared to carrying so much luggage around with us.

Similarly, the emotional baggage you are carrying is interfering with your enjoyment of the trip called life. If you go to a party, you are carrying the emotional pain; if you are invited to take a promotion at work, you are carrying the emotional pain; if you start a new relationship, you are carrying the emotional pain. Everywhere you turn, you have one of those bags strapped to you, making it difficult to function.

Unless you deal with the pain from your past head-on, it will be going with you everywhere—and probably keep you from experiencing the true joy your life could offer.

Several years ago, I met a young man to whom I agreed to give pastoral advice and direction. He was married with a son and having lots of problems in his marriage, at work when he had a job, with his family, and so on. Virtually, every area of this young man's life was in disarray. As I began to work with him, it became very apparent that his life mirrored my own in many ways. He had been abused by a stepfather, abandoned by a biological father, talked down to, knocked around, and spoken to like an unwanted human being. He turned to drugs, drinking, and violence as a mechanism to cope with his past, and in some way, mask his intense emotions with the temporary high those activities offered. By the time we met, he was desperately trying to make his life work with his wife, who was running out of patience. Each time he took a step forward, it seemed like he was taking two backwards. He would go to counseling, do okay for a while, and then return to his old ways. He would go to church looking for spiritual guidance, do okay for a while, and then return to his old ways. He would make up his mind that enough was enough, do okay for a while, and then return to his old ways. He was definitely carrying the luggage of pain with him everywhere.

As I began to work with him, I noticed that every time we spoke about the previous week's events, he would unveil his failing for the week and then blame his past as the culprit that made him do it. Each week, we would assign him a new task to help overcome his challenges, and each week, he would return with another story of failure. We worked on communication skills, coping skills, anger management skills, and many others. I tried to equip his wife with tools she could use to communicate with him better and to help him through periods of struggle. Nothing seemed to help. He continued this pattern for several months, along the way fighting with bosses and coworkers, arguing with police officers, and ending up in jail. The entire situation was really tough on his family and his children.

What became very evident was that he carried baggage with him from every disappointment in his past at all times. Every altercation with his father he would put in a new bag; every time he was talked about, he put that in a new bag; even self-inflicted disappointments he would put in new bags. My young friend was carrying so many bags of pain with him that he couldn't see the pathway in front of him or the sky above him. His vision was totally blocked by all this luggage he insisted on carrying.

How many bags are you carrying with you? Are they getting so heavy that it is difficult to see your future? Has someone hurt you in such a way that you are carrying that pain with you today?

Take a moment to write down each piece of luggage you are carrying. What are some of the situations, big or small, that have you weighed down?

_____   _____
_____   _____
_____   _____
_____   _____
_____   _____
_____   _____

CHOOSING YOUR HEALING

After years of carrying this pain from your past, I am sure you are ready to release it. It's time to unpack your luggage and choose healing. After several years of being angry at my situation, being frustrated that it had happened to me, wallowing in self-pity based on my circumstances, and limiting my thinking to the edge of my pain, I had to move on. It was time to move beyond my pain and walk in power, passion, and success. I chose healing, and you can too.

So how do you choose healing? What is the process to get to the place where this stuff doesn't bother you any longer? The answer lies in the conclusion of my young friend's story.

As I stated, it became abundantly clear that my young friend was carrying around tremendous amounts of luggage full of his past pains. One day, during one of our sessions, he was telling me the story of his latest escapade and how he had fallen victim to circumstances; as usual, he stated that the world was against him and no one would allow him to succeed in his plight to be healed and "normal." After nearly thirty minutes of listening intently as I had done on several occasions, it hit me that my friend didn't realize that living in this pain was a choice. He hadn't chosen what had happened, but he certainly was choosing to live there. At this point in my own life, I had taken the necessary steps to gain healing from my own pain. I had unpacked my luggage a long time ago and realized that I would not let the pain from my past define who I would be or become. At the time of this conversation, I had a successful career as a regional manager for a large bank, I was speaking at churches across our state, leading several ministries in our local church, and working with people like my young friend to help them restore their lives. My friend saw me as a sort of mentor, but I had never told him about the pain I had lived through.

So I stopped him and said, "You know, you have a choice to live this way or not. Every day, you choose whether to stay in this pain or rise above it." Somewhat frustrated with my response, he gave me a look that begged for an explanation. I went on to tell him my story. I helped him to understand that he and I had walked the same path and experienced the same things in our younger years. Yet I was giving him advice and he was living in complete dysfunction. The only difference between us was that I had chosen not to be defined by my past while he hadn't made that choice. From that period on, he was never the same. Realizing that someone he respected and trusted had lived through the same thing and could make the choice to have a successful career, a loving wife, peace in his home, and to be on the road to financial freedom was overwhelming, but encouraging to him at the same time.

My young friend and I then began the process of getting him to choose to be healed of his past pain. We started unpacking the luggage right there, bag by bag, until he was making the choice to live a life free from that pain.

I realize it hurts! I know it's painful! But the truth is that you are choosing to keep it or move beyond it. By keeping it, you are giving more power to your abuser than that person deserves. He or she tried to control you and hurt you, and living with that pain allows him or her to win. Quite frankly, that was not acceptable to me, and it shouldn't be to you either.

The process to choose healing requires five steps:

1. **Recognize It:** This may seem relatively self-explanatory, but the truth is that in many cases, anger, frustration, confusion, and dysfunction stem from pain from your past, and yet not once have you recognized the connection. Often, I can meet someone who suffers from any number of the above symptoms, and with a bit of exploration, find that somewhere in that person's past was a tragic or horrific event. I know in my own situation, I realized that I was angry, frustrated, and embarrassed, but I thought I was strong enough to handle the things that had happened to me. I eventually associated the emotion with its

cause, which needs to be done. The faster you recognize it, the faster you can heal from it.

2. **Confess It:** I stated in my personal story that my mother was oblivious to what was happening to me. She had no idea what my stepfather was doing or that I was in a horrible situation. That's the M.O. (*modus operandi*) for abusers; they are masters of hiding what they are doing. I "handled" this pain, masked it by attempting to overachieve, joined the military to escape it, fought constantly with my father in hopes of hurting him like he hurt me, but it wasn't until I talked about it that I began to gain the strength to overcome it. An old maxim says, "Confession is good for the soul." I truly believe that. As I began to talk about it and confess it, I was building up strength to deal with it and eventually overcome it. The pain no longer had control of me; I was in control of it. Find someone you trust so you can begin sharing your story. A Bible verse comes to mind here: "You overcome by the blood of the lamb and the word of your testimony" (Revelation 12:11). Overcoming happens through the word of your testimony.

3. **Forgive It:** I remember studying the Scriptures and coming across the verse, "But if you do not forgive men their trespasses, neither will your Father forgive your trespasses" (Matthew 6:15). Quite shocking to someone with the amount of pain and frustration I had pent up inside me. "Forgive?" I thought. "How on earth do I do that?" So often we believe that "forgive" equals "forget," and I didn't see that happening. To some extent, I believed that if I were to forgive, I was in some way telling my abuser that it was okay to have hurt me that way. My mind began to assess what implications there would be to forgiving. Did it somehow mean that I was a co-conspirator? Did it mean that I had asked for it or given permission for these things to take place? What I learned is that forgiving actually releases

me from the connection to my abuser. Forgiveness allows me to move beyond his control, beyond his abuse, beyond the memory of his terror. Forgiving him was more about me than about him. It was telling my heart that I don't hold contempt or vengeance against him for his actions. Similarly, Jesus asked God to forgive those who tortured and crucified him by saying, "They know not what they do." This forgiveness released His heart to be free from them. Forgiveness allows you to let go of the grudges, bitterness, and contempt you are holding in those bags for the person who hurt you. Forgiving what happened doesn't mean forgetting it. It simply releases your heart to move on.

4. **Heal It:** At some point in your life, you have probably had a sore that you kept picking at, only to realize that it wasn't healing. It wasn't until you stopped touching it and messing with it that it really began to heal. Just like a cut needs to be free from your constant touching, your emotional pain needs the same thing. Leave it alone! Now that you have exposed it by confessing it to someone, leave it alone. Let the healing process take place and your heart gain strength. So many of us want to keep petting our wounds and playing with them from fear we may not have an identity separate from them. My young friend and I made a commitment that he would no longer use his pain as an excuse to act up or act out. Each day's decisions became based on the emotions, occurrences, and actions he took for that day. He had to let it go and let it heal.

5. **Make the Choice:** Every day, make the choice to be healed. You have the right to choose how you feel, how you act, what you respond to, what decisions you make, and the course of your day. Having a bad day or a good day is your choice. Living in your pain and hurt is your choice. Giving some abuser power over you is a choice. Choose to be healthy emotionally and to walk away from that pain. I realize this sounds easy, and I also

realize it is not easy. But it is possible. You don't have to define your life as a victim; you can choose to be a victor! No matter what happens to you, good or bad, your response is a choice. Choose health!

Now that you know the five steps for healing, go back to the earlier list you made of all of the luggage you are carrying around. Pick the one you most want to work on, and apply the five steps to it. Repeat the process for each piece of luggage until you are free from all your baggage.

1. **Realize It:** What is the piece of luggage?

2. **Forgive It:** Seek to Forgive: Write out a forgiveness statement, or if safe, tell the person you forgive him or her if appropriate.

3. **Confess It:** Whom can you tell about your piece of luggage to help you overcome it?

4. **Heal It:** Now that you are aware of the problem and have forgiven the wrongdoer, work on letting it go. When the thought of that luggage arises, shift your thoughts away from it so you quit focusing on it. Remember, you can't heal a sore by continuing to pick at it.

5. **Make the Choice:** Choose to be healed from this problem so you no longer have to carry it around.

OVERCOMING THE PAIN—FOREVER

Understand that what I have just described is not a onetime fix so all is good for the rest of your life. You still maintain your memories, and some of them are not very healthy or positive. Overcoming the Pain Forever means that for the rest of your life, you must choose life over death, power over powerlessness, healing over pain. You are an overcomer regardless of how you might feel or how someone else decides to treat you today.

Remember who you are and what you have overcome as your vision begins to gain clarity. Overcoming this vision blocker is significant for moving your life forward and seeing the amazing possibilities that lie ahead.

My young friend has been growing tremendously over the past several years. Since our revelation regarding his need to make a choice and his successfully completing the process, his marriage is thriving, he is doing great work at his job, his kids are fantastic, and he is sharing hope with other people. When I recently asked him how the process was going, he responded, "Every day I make the choice, and every day I win." Overcoming the Pain Forever means that you commit for the rest of your life to making the choice to live in a state of healing!

SUMMARY

Pain from our past is very real and debilitating. It keeps us from moving forward and blocks any sort of vision we may have. Truthfully, you can't see beyond the pain to get a glimpse of a vision. But you don't have to live that way any longer. Healing the pain of your past allows you the freedom to conquer anything and live a powerful life with great relationships.

The choice is yours! What will you do with today? Can you make the decision to recognize it, confess it, forgive it, heal it, and choose to move on? Only by doing so will you be able to rid yourself of the shame and anger that tries to keep you locked down and ineffective. You can do it! I know there is a life on the other side of the pain because I'm living there now.

CHAPTER 8

Choosing a Healthy Lifestyle

"Physical fitness is not only one of the most important keys
to a healthy body; it is the basis of dynamic and
creative intellectual activity."
— John F. Kennedy

It started in the summer of 2008, just before my wife and I were leaving for our annual conference in Veracruz, Mexico. Each year we are invited there for a week in the late summer to speak at a pastors and leaders conference. It is always a great trip and one we look forward to taking. Some of our greatest friends lead some of the best churches and outreach ministries in the state of Veracruz. The 2008 trip, however, was very different; Saundra began to have pain in her body, nausea continually, and severe headaches that she couldn't seem to alleviate. She was a trooper, however, and decided to make the trip anyway. We traveled, taught, and spent time with our friends, but all the while, Saundra was suffering from inexplicable pains and strange happenings in her body. As pastors of a small church with no other income to speak of, we tried home remedies, pain medications, prayer, and many other things just to relieve her pain. Over time, the symptoms grew worse, leaving her debilitated and unable to leave bed on some days while on others, she functioned just fine, or so it seemed. She would say that things weren't too bad and would allow herself the indulgence of being with friends or sharing in a meal. I have to say that watching my wife go through this has affirmed for me that she is the strongest person I know. Over time, we spent money on research, doctors, tests, and different remedies, but nothing was ever concluded about the cause of her pain. Doctors would tell her they knew something was wrong; they just didn't know what.

Saundra would have long periods where she only had minor symptoms, and then all of a sudden, the entirety of her pain and nausea would come rushing back like a raging river in a flood. It was never too far away. Frustrated by the doctors' responses, Saundra went on a quest to find solutions to her issues. She read about many possible diagnoses based on similar symptoms to her condition; it seemed she could have had any number of diseases, ailments, or health issues, but none seemed to explain everything, and trying the remedies left her perplexed and frustrated.

February of 2011 would change our household forever. Saundra was discussing her symptoms with a friend when they collectively determined that perhaps she was suffering from a dairy allergy that caused neurological issues. Neither was a medical doctor, but together they found information that explained the majority of her issues. When Saundra had herself tested for food allergies, some conclusive evidence was found to explain many of her ailments. She began to monitor the foods we ate, eliminated dairy from our diet, began to consume large amounts of water, and was relentless at watching what we ate. Miraculously, her symptoms began to disappear. She had lost a huge amount of weight, but now she was returning to a healthy weight. The next six months began a recovery period for her body that continues to this date. This experience made us realize the power of healthy living and the importance of monitoring what goes in our bodies and how we treat them.

Failure to live a healthy lifestyle is a significant vision blocker. If your body is not functioning correctly, your vision won't either. In our fast food society, we have to make an extra effort to ensure our bodies live and last long.

GARBAGE IN, GARBAGE OUT

When I was learning about computers, my instructors would state "Garbage in, Garbage out" in reference to the kind of information you feed the computer. If you feed the computer bad information, it will produce bad results. Garbage in, Garbage out. This same concept holds true with our bodies. When we put garbage in, garbage comes out.

We want our bodies to perform optimally. We want them to do more, go farther, last longer, and be more agile than ever before. Our technology-based society has created longer work weeks and allowed us to produce more in a day than ever before. To get to our vision and create the life we want, it's up to us to have a body that will get us there.

On any given day, what are you putting in your body? What are the chemicals, hormone-infused, modified, processed foods you allow to pass your lips and enter the most important system you have?

We should ask these questions when concerned about weight loss and poor health. I realize I am not a nutritionist or a medical doctor, but I do understand that what goes in affects positively or negatively what comes out. I recommend you consult your doctor before beginning any new diet or plan.

One October, I was feeling extremely sluggish, my brain was foggy, and I couldn't seem to get enough sleep. I would go to bed at 9 p.m., sleep until 6 a.m., and wake as tired as I went to bed. Something was definitely wrong. I wasn't feeling sick; I just seemed not to function. I went to my doctor, who ran a battery of tests. The results concluded that my body was not functioning optimally because I was deficient in several vitamins and my diet was not adding any value. I was diet drained! My doctor prescribed a list of vitamins, minerals, and a proper diet and eating schedule to put me back on track.

Fundamentally, her plan was very simple:

1. Take the supplements
2. Eat five smaller meals per day
3. Limit fat intake and eat lean protein
4. Eliminate sugar and add vegetables
5. Drink lots of water
6. Exercise

Basically, she wanted me to eliminate all the garbage that was going in and replace it with good healthy food that would fuel my body and allow it to perform at a very high level.

This situation forced me to take a look at what I was putting in my body. Even with Saundra's efforts to eliminate dairy and other processed type foods, it seemed I continued to consume unhealthy food. Making the changes she suggested have kept me feeling fantastic.

What are you putting in your body? For the next seven days, write down what you consume. You will be amazed by the kinds of things you put in, expecting a great outcome.

MONDAY	TUESDAY	WEDNESDAY	THURSDAY	FRIDAY	SATURDAY	SUNDAY
Breakfast						
Lunch						
Dinner						
Snack						

List the kinds of snacks you like   What fruits could replace them?

_____   _____

_____   _____

_____   _____

We live in a fast food driven society. Tremendous demands on our time cause us to rush to work, then to kid's practices, and then to evening meetings. We have calls to return, a household to manage, chores to accomplish, and then we get up and do it all again the next day. Fast food becomes our quick solution to cooking at home. We can pick up take out and be on our way in a matter of minutes, saving precious time we believe can better be spent on other things. Don't misunderstand me; I am not recommending this alternative. I'm merely pointing out the rationale we use to justify fast food for our families. While we may all enjoy the occasional hamburger, and it's understandable that fast food will play some role in our lives, it should not be the primary source for our families.

So many resources are available today to help structure a good eating plan. Search them out, but also begin with some simple things right now: eliminate sugar and replace it with fruits and vegetables; change from soda and carbonated drinks to water, lots of water; add servings of vegetables to your diet on a regular basis; and don't make every night pizza night. These simple changes will help you begin losing weight and feeling great. Our bodies are starving for good stuff to go in so good stuff can come out.

Don't forget to exercise. While exercise may not be something we put in our bodies, it certainly optimizes it. Exercise has so many great effects. It reduces stress, lowers blood pressure, builds strong muscles and bones, and burns calories, which allows you to lose weight and keep it off, thereby reducing the chance of heart attack and diabetes.

The Mayo Clinic reports seven benefits of regular physical activity:

1. Exercise controls weight
2. Exercise combats health conditions
3. Exercise improves mood
4. Exercise boosts energy
5. Exercise promotes better sleep
6. Exercise puts the spark back in your sex life
7. Exercise can be fun

Exercise should be a regular part of your daily life plan. Studies suggest that twenty minutes a day can vastly improve your energy and reduce your chances of heart-related diseases. My plan with my doctor involves a full sixty minutes each day. Activities like walking, biking, running, going to the gym, and doing sit-ups and stretches at home are all good ways to change your routine and make exercise fun.

Admittedly, some of the best thinking I do happens when I am at the gym. There I'm free from the regular distractions: no cell phone ringing, no TV playing, and no questions coming at me—just me and the treadmill or the weights. I can focus my mind and gain clarity on situations and decisions required of me. Exercise allows your body to raise its metabolism and burn more calories while allowing your mind to become sharp and crisp.

Exercise doesn't have to be complicated. So many of us put so much pressure on ourselves to have this rigid workout routine, but really, all your body is craving is movement and activity that elevates your heart rate. Do something fun like going for a walk with your spouse, run a short obstacle course, play some basketball with the guys/girls, go to the beach and walk its length. Once you start, your body will begin to crave exercise, driving your energy levels through the roof and your weight through the floor.

Take a few minutes and come up with three activities you love to do that could be used as part of your workout routine.

1. _____
2. _____
3. _____

CHOOSING TO BE HEALTHY

Sluggish and lethargic bodies don't produce the greatest vision. Poor health, bad eating habits, and addictive behaviors all play a major role in blocking your vision, primarily because you are too tired to give it much effort. Vision is blocked simply because the body is lacking the fuel to produce it and sustain it. But making the decision to be healthy is a choice. You can choose to change your lifestyle and become healthy, or you can choose to continue the abuse to your body and ignore the issue. Either way, it's a choice.

While I don't have much time for television, one of my favorite shows to watch with Saundra is *The Biggest Loser*. This reality show brings together people from all walks of life, rich or poor, celebrity or non-celebrity, parent or teen, all of them severely overweight, and takes them through a process of healing and healthy living. Throughout the episodes, you watch transformation after transformation of contestants changing their lives by learning the habits of healthy eating and exercise. The trainers each have a different style for working with their teams, but one thing is extremely consistent: they bring each contestant face-to-face with the reality that he or she has a CHOICE! It's up to each one to make the conscious decision to live healthy and work out. The contestants' ultimate goal is not to win a prize but to win a life. They have to choose to go through the process and change.

The same is true with you and me. Just like my young friend in the last chapter had to choose to deal with the pain of his past, we must choose to deal with healthy living. Every day we choose how we are going to live and what we are going to accept. I realize the easy thing to do is choose not to change, but I challenge you to make the choice to live healthily. Make good choices to eliminate bad things from your diet and lifestyle and replace them with good ones.

Here is a list of things you can choose to remove and why you should:

1. **Smoking:** Smoking kills over 400,000 Americans each year

2. **Drinking Alcohol:** Alcohol damages brain and body cells and has a very high chemical content, causing it to be very addictive

3. **Lack of Proper Sleep:** Sleep allows the body to regenerate and replaces vital functions

4. **Chemical Abuse:** Chemicals just damage your body all the way around

5. **Staying Overweight:** Causes diabetes, heart disease, and high blood pressure

6. **Drinking Coffee:** Coffee is full of caffeine, which addicts the body and depletes energy

7. **Sugar:** Creates high and low mood swings and is overall unhealthy

8. **Soft Drinks:** High in chemicals and caffeine, and the carbonation depletes oxygen

9. **Overeating:** Overloads your body with calories

10. **Eating Junk Food:** Causes weight gain and many other issues

You can choose to keep these things in your life or to remove them. I challenge you to remove them and do something else instead: read a book, go to the gym, make a diet plan full of good foods and vegetables, find alternatives to drinking alcohol and soft drinks, like water.

Make the choice right now to change your health habits. The key is one thing at a time. If you try to tackle everything at once, it becomes overwhelming and you set yourself up for defeat.

Write down one thing you can tackle and make the choice to remove or change it. Focus on it for the next thirty days and then add another.

What one thing can you change?

_____

CREATING A HEALTHY LIFESTYLE

3 John 1:2 says, "Beloved, I pray that you may prosper in all things and be in health, just as your soul prospers." God designed your body to operate in perfect harmony and with precision. Your body was created like a well-oiled machine designed to do so much, but it won't run right without proper use and regular maintenance.

How do you create a healthy lifestyle? Having spent years creating a poor environment, what does one need to do to turn the situation around?

Taking the following four steps will create a healthy lifestyle for you:

1. **Make It a Priority:** Many people wait until they receive some tragic diagnosis from their doctor before making a healthy lifestyle a priority. The truth is you will do what is important to you. Excuse after excuse can be given, and believe me I have tried them all. I don't have time, it's too hard, I don't know what to do, I have never worked out before and don't know my way around the gym, and I am embarrassed to be seen at the gym looking like this. None of these excuses are valid; they simply stand in the way of everything you are trying to accomplish in your life. Health is imperative and will allow you to love what you do so much more. But you have to make it the priority. Decide that a healthy lifestyle is important to you and it will become a priority you begin to spend time working on.

   Priorities are things you plan for, create, schedule around, and invest in. If I were to look at your checkbook register for the past month, we would begin to see what is important to you. Entertainment, dining out, educational activities, and clothes might all be on the list, based on what you have invested. We could do the same with your calendar over the past week. You will schedule what is important to you.

   Making a healthy lifestyle a priority will begin to shift your calendar, your spending, and your creative thinking. Once it becomes a priority, you will find yourself thinking about how it fits into your schedule.

2. **Know the Purpose:** Why are you making the change to create a healthy lifestyle? You are reading this book to learn how to remove obstacles to your destiny and health issues are one of those obstacles. You want to prevent heart disease, and you want to feel better, look better, do more, and accomplish more. Figure out the reason why you want those things—the purpose of your transformation will fuel the transformation. Job 22:28

says, "Declare a thing, and it will be established for you; so your light will shine on your ways." I love this verse because it is so true. Say what you want and why you want it. Make the declaration! "I am going to live healthily so I can live my dreams." "I am going to live healthily so I can make more money, enjoy my family, etc." Make your declaration and know why you are making this change.

Imagine yourself making the declaration, having it established in your life, and seeing the light illuminate your path. See yourself accomplishing this mission, the mission you established, not for your husband, wife, kids, mother, father, or anyone else. The mission you established for you. Make your declaration today and know your purpose!

3. **Create the Plan:** What gets planned gets done. Luke 14:28 says, "For which of you, desiring to build a tower, does not first sit down and count the cost, whether he has enough to complete it? Otherwise, when he has laid a foundation, he will not be able to finish." Making it a priority and knowing your purpose are essential, but making the plan puts this creation into action. I love this quote: "Planning without action is futile; action without planning is fatal."

In order to create a healthy lifestyle, you must make a plan that encompasses three areas:

- Nutrition: Work with someone in your community or your doctor to address this topic.

- Exercise: Get it going and plan what you will do each day.

- Lifestyle Choices: Plan your TV time, Facebook time, schedule some reading, but you must manage your lifestyle choices as part of your plan. Creating a plan will allow you to take the stress and worry out of your decisions. Take some time on Sunday evening to plan your week: your workout schedule, your meals, your entertainment choices, and so on. Planning will allow you to begin changing your lifestyle to support and promote health.

4. **Gain Persistence:** Don't Quit! You can do this! Get angry, upset, and mad at your current situation. Do whatever it takes to drive you to a place of passion burning so strong that you will keep going. Persistence is a remarkable quality. It moves beyond talent, goes further than skill, and surpasses intellect. Persistence takes average people and makes them extraordinary. When you gain persistence, you gain a sense of drive that will keep you moving despite any obstacle that gets in your way. You drive right through feelings, emotions, irritations, and naysayers to the place of success and right past your goal. Gain persistence to achieve a new way of living.

SUMMARY

A number of years ago, I realized I needed to get my body in shape. A voice inside told me I was headed somewhere great and that I had to be ready mentally, intellectually, spiritually, and physically. I believe I had a mandate to live healthily to achieve the goals being placed before me. I realized my life is not my own. I have been designed to help others and lend a hand where I can. Giving time, talent, and resources to help others who are struggling or less fortunate than me is a calling I don't take lightly. To accomplish that goal requires a healthy lifestyle and healthy choices.

By taking control of your health and giving your body the chance to function at athletically optimized levels, you can begin to see what may be your life's purpose. For too long now, our bodies have been subjected to fast food, chemically based drinks, caffeine, sugar, and countless other deterioration-causing substances. It's time to take our health back and unlock the energy, power, and vision that our bodies have been too tired to produce. Choose to be healthy; choose to make a change!

CHAPTER 9

Connecting Correctly

"There are essentially two things that will make you wise—the books you read and the people you meet."

— Jack Canfield

To this point, you have been learning mostly about internal Vision Blockers. Each one has dealt with a certain condition of the heart or mind or both that affects your ability to gain clarity on your vision. From fear to double-mindedness, these vision blockers represent internal struggles and conflicts that prevent vision from growing out of your heart. In this chapter, we will discover an outward vision blocker with the same stifling power as the internal ones.

Relationships can have a profound effect on your life and vision. Whom you connect with and how will largely determine your level of success or lack thereof. Relationships are powerful, valuable, and enrich a life, bringing so much color and experience that would not be gained if you were to live this life alone. Each relationship offers you the opportunity to learn through the experiences you have with that person. Some relationships give you a much needed push while others pull you back and keep you from moving forward. Determining which is which and how to engage each differently will allow you the freedom to explore your vision and passion in greater depth.

Let's face it; we all have relationships in our lives. People are a very large part of doing anything. You find people at work, whether they be coworkers, direct reports, superiors, customers, or support people. You find people at the grocery store, in the park, or at the entertainment establishments you frequent. There are people at church and in clubs you support. Now there are people online in any number of social media sites: your Facebook friends (who may or may not be your friends), Twitter, LinkedIn, Pinterest, Instagram, etc. There are people everywhere requesting your time and attention. The question becomes: How do you connect correctly? Where do you spend your time? Are there friends who are friends and friends who are not?

In this chapter, we are going to discuss connecting correctly. We'll take a look at the relationships you keep and the ones you don't with the idea that some of these relationships are actually blocking your vision and keeping you from your destiny.

PLACING VALUE ON PEOPLE

To evaluate our relationships properly, first we need to establish a foundation from which to build. So let's begin with a mutual understanding that people are valuable and have incredible worth. All people have value! Jesus was very clear when he said, "Love your neighbor as yourself." He was teaching us that we must place as high a value on our neighbor's life as we do on our own. The Scriptures go on to tell us in Philippians 2:3 to "esteem others above ourselves." These passages remind us of our obligation to value people, knowing that each one has a gift, a purpose, and potential to offer this world. Self-preservation and self-promoting come naturally to most people, whereas promoting others is a foreign concept and hard to grasp. Selfishness isn't a far journey, but selflessness is a lifelong hike.

People are the priority. Releasing your vision will ultimately be about how you live your life to impact others' lives. The services you provide, the coaching you do, the products you sell, the relationships you have, the people you enlist will all be about impacting other people's lives and enriching them in some way. In his book *It's Not Just Who You Know,* Tommy Spaulding says that most companies focus on ROI or Return on Investment when true value comes to an organization by focusing on ROR or Return on Relationships. He proposes that by investing in relationships and creating a culture where relationships are considered the most valuable commodity you have, your company will gain market share and heart share from its clients and potential clients. He further explains that people do business with people, and more importantly, they do business with people they care about and people who care about them.

Without doubt, relationships are important and the people in those relationships carry tremendous value. They can propel you forward and help you reach your goal, or they can bring you down and keep you from reaching anything at all. The difference lies in connecting correctly.

THROWING JONAH OVERBOARD

While there is value in people, not every relationship serves you, your life, or your vision in a positive way. Just as some relationships will propel you to levels you haven't seen before, others are unhealthy and will keep you from achieving your dream or seeing your vision fulfilled. How do you determine whom you should connect with and whom you should have exit your life?

An Old Testament story full of drama that reads like a novel with action, anticipation, and intrigue is the story of Jonah and his disobedience when God called him to deliver a life-changing message. God told Jonah to go to the city of Nineveh and preach repentance to the wicked people. Jonah, however, did not want to fulfill this mission because he didn't believe the people deserved the redirection and inspiration that would allow them to rise above their current circumstances. Jonah rebelled and decided to do his own thing by paying a fare and boarding a ship headed in the opposite direction. God was not happy with his disobedience, as revealed in the following passage:

> But the Lord sent out a great wind on the sea, and there was a mighty tempest on the sea, so that the ship was about to be broken up. Then the mariners were afraid; and every man cried out to his god, and threw the cargo that was in the ship into the sea, to lighten the load. But Jonah had gone down into the lowest parts of the ship, had lain down, and was fast asleep. So the captain came to him, and said to him, "What do you mean, sleeper? Arise, call on your God; perhaps your God will consider us, so that we may not perish." And they said to one another, "Come, let us cast lots, that we may know for whose cause this trouble has come upon us." So they cast lots, and the lot fell on Jonah. Then they said to him, "Please tell us! For whose cause is this trouble upon us? What is your occupation? And where do you come from? What is your country? And of what people are you?" So he said to them, "I am a Hebrew; and I fear the Lord, the God of heaven, who made the sea and the dry land." Then the men were exceedingly afraid, and said to him, "Why have you done this?" For the men knew that he fled from the

presence of the Lord, because he had told them. Then they said to him, "What shall we do to you that the sea may be calm for us?"—for the sea was growing more tempestuous. And he said to them, "Pick me up and throw me into the sea; then the sea will become calm for you. For I know that this great tempest is because of me." Nevertheless the men rowed hard to return to land, but they could not, for the sea continued to grow more tempestuous against them. Therefore they cried out to the Lord and said, "We pray, O Lord, please do not let us perish for this man's life, and do not charge us with innocent blood; for You, O Lord, have done as it pleased You." So they picked up Jonah and threw him into the sea, and the sea ceased from its raging. (Jonah 1:4-15)

In order to save their lives, the mariners' only solution was to throw Jonah overboard. Obviously, we are not going to toss people off a ship's deck, but we can exit them from our lives, or at minimum, keep them from having authority or voice to speak to our destiny. Figuratively speaking, "throwing someone overboard" in this chapter means you have determined that person is no longer allowed to keep you from your destiny or block your vision.

In this story, Jonah was the culprit keeping the mariners from reaching their destination of Tarshish. What would have been an otherwise profitable journey was thwarted by Jonah when he boarded the ship. He brought with him characteristics that were not in the mariners' best interests and even proved to be disturbing, dangerous, and disastrous. Jonah had completely walked away from his vision and life's mission, and now his very presence caused those around him trouble.

Think about the people you have allowed to board the ship of your life. There may be some like Jonah whom you can determine, without question, it is time to "throw overboard." But most of the time, the determination of which ones should exit is more difficult.

Let's look at the four characteristics of Jonah's life that disqualified him as the right person to keep on the ship:

1. **Jonah was Rebellious:** Jonah recognized the calling that was placed on his life. He knew the instructions he had from God to go to Nineveh and help those people out of their misery and terrible situation, but because of his personal disdain for the Ninevites, he chose to go his own way and do his own thing. He was a "rebel without a cause." Being rebellious means "showing open opposition toward a person or group in authority." Jonah was rebellious toward the good things in his life, toward the place of purpose, and toward the calling placed on his life—all for the sake of doing what felt right for him or gratified his personal pleasure. You probably have someone like that in your life. A person who just will not do right or make right decisions. He is constantly trying to buck the system or fight for his plight, no matter how futile it may be. In some situations, being rebellious can be admirable, but not when people rebel solely for the sake of rebellion. The rationale of such people really doesn't line up with a personal conviction or value system. They simply won't do something because someone told them to do it. In fact, they will typically do the opposite just as a matter of principle.

Rebellious people always try to get you to fight their fight. Allowing rebellious people on your boat will cause you great heartache and frustration. You will find yourself fighting fights just to fight instead of passionately fighting to move a cause forward. You really have to be careful because in many cases the logic of these people seems sound. You become impassioned by their plight against all those who tell them what to do. You begin to redirect your efforts to rebel against the conspiracy when really there is no conspiracy. Furthermore, rebellious people typically reject traditional values and defy moral conviction. They have very little, if any, appreciation for authority, and their value is placed on doing whatever they want to do, whatever the cost.

Years can be lost, damage can be done, and vision can be sacrificed by allowing rebellious people to gain a voice in your life.

Who are the rebellious people in your life? List the ones who are steering you off course and the ones whose cause you find yourself fighting for instead of your own.

_____   _____

_____   _____

2. **Jonah was Negative:** Jonah did not believe the people of Nineveh could or would change. He would much rather have sentenced the city to destruction than offer a solution for the people's recovery from their poor decisions and wicked ways. Jonah did not have a positive attitude toward the city's redemption, and that negativity drove him to flee from his calling.

   Nothing is more depressing than to be around someone who always has something negative to say about someone or something. Looking at the worst-case scenario, viewing things from the dark side of the mountain, or just simply having a negative opinion about the future or the plan breeds doubt and confusion. One of the main issues with having a negative person's voice in your life is that it's easier to believe the negative than the positive. Most of us spend our lives dealing with a tremendous amount of insecurity and doubt about our capabilities and talents. We already believe it will be difficult to achieve our dream, our passion, and our vision, so when we hear the negative, it serves only to confirm what we were thinking in the first place.

Negative voices speak louder than positive ones, so it's time to "toss them overboard." A vision is waiting to be birthed in your life, but negative voices stifle its development. You have been designed with a calling and a purpose that will transform your financial circumstances, your relationships, your family, and the world around you. How do I know? Because you decided to read this book and eliminate the blockers from that vision. That alone tells me something is stirring inside of you and waiting to erupt. Negative voices will tell you that your dream is silly, you don't have the capacity to achieve, or you aren't talented enough to accomplish anything. The truth is that their opinions don't really matter.

Those voices need to be silenced and the negative people in your life need to be tossed overboard. They are causing the storms in your life to blow with a fierce wind and giving room for you to doubt your ultimate goal. Jonah looked at the deliverance of Nineveh as a pipe dream, something that could never be accomplished in his lifetime. But the end of the story tells us that once Jonah finally went and executed on his calling, the whole city was transformed and became quite productive.

Eliminating the negative people from your life will allow you the freedom to pursue your vision and dream with passion. You already have to fight your internal insecurity, so why fight someone else's?

Who are the negative voices in your life? What voices continue to tell you that you can't do it or don't have what it takes?

_____   _____

_____   _____

3. **Jonah was Insecurity-Driven:** The primary driver for Jonah's rebellion was he believed the task was impossible and that he didn't possess the talent, skill, or faith to accomplish the assignment. He was gripped by fear of the overwhelming responsibility, and the size of the task was too much for him to rationalize in his mind. He became acutely aware of his own limitations and insecurity began to drive his decision.

   The impact an insecure person can have on your life is amazing. Insecurity is present in so many lives that it's like a highly contagious disease without a known antidote. Insecurity plagues lives, drives decisions, and destroys relationships all in one fell swoop. You can imagine why you wouldn't want an insecure person on your ship when you are trying to release vision and make life-impacting changes. Insecure people say, "You can't do it" because they wouldn't do it.

   Insecurity is so widespread that to try eliminating insecure people from your life would be a futile and unproductive effort. Cruel in fact! Insecure people need reinforcement and encouragement to rise above insecurity. While we should be compassionate toward the insecure and help them, we don't need to let their insecurity drive our decisions or speak to our vision.

   The issue with insecurity as it relates to you and your vision is found in its common characteristics:

   - Insecurity rarely allows for celebration of another person's success. Compliments are not on the tip of the tongue for most insecure people, and therefore, they find themselves criticizing before complimenting.

- Insecurity requires the host always to be right and have the final word on everything. Collaboration doesn't really come into play because the insecure person believes he is right and will ensure that he has the final word on any matter. Your opinion isn't nearly as valuable as his.

- The insecure person limits others' opportunities. Your advancement is not celebrated because it causes the insecure person to be threatened by your success. If you go up in some way, it translates to the insecure person going down.

- An insecure person typically makes a joke of everything or finds humor in "slamming" another person. If the insecure person can discredit you or joke about your success, that causes emphasis to be diverted from him to you, which temporarily relieves his anxiety.

The truth is that insecure people need love, care, admonishment, and direction. More often than not, their insecurity will not allow them to gain access to help. While their insecurity is tragic for them, it doesn't and shouldn't keep you from achieving your dream or executing on your vision. Allowing others' insecurities to have a say in your life will cause you to make decisions that do not move you toward your goal.

Who are the insecure people to whom you've given a voice? Identify the people who, going forward, need limited access to your dream and vision.

_____   _____

_____   _____

4. **Jonah Did Not Believe:** Jonah did not believe that Nineveh could turn around and be a productive, wholesome city. He doubted the possibilities that lay ahead for this city and its people. This lack of belief caused him to work against the plan for its future.

So often, we listen to people who don't believe in us. Nothing blocks a vision like someone telling you that you can't do it or you won't do it. While outrageous power exists in hearing someone tell you how successful you can be or how proud he or she is of your accomplishments (a topic we will cover further in a moment), the same is true of those who tell you the opposite—that your dream is silly, unrealistic, or even foolish. Those voices do more damage than good and only serve to limit you from achieving all for which you have been designed.

What I've learned in my life is that some people support and champion you while others pull you down. The key is to eliminate the ones who pull you down. I have been blessed to have several people in my life who encourage me and believe in what I am doing or where I'm going. My life has also been plagued by the occasional naysayer or doubting Thomas. For several years, I allowed the naysaying voices to be the dominant sound in my ear. At the time, it seemed more plausible that my ideas were ridiculous and farfetched. Listening to those voices only affirmed the doubt I had already conceived in my own heart.

Not until I realized those voices were keeping me bound in mediocrity and average performance, and that they were wrong and my dreams did have value, did my vision gain momentum and self-confidence begin to overtake my life.

Throw the voices of disbelief overboard. They should have no voice in your life. While prudent counsel is wise naysaying, disbelief is not acceptable within an earshot of me.

Who represents that disbelief in your life? Which people continue to tell you that you can't do it?

_____   _____

_____   _____

What characteristics from Jonah do you possess now that you are willing to "throw overboard"?

_____   _____

_____   _____

These four characteristics—Rebelliousness, Negativity, Insecurity-Driven, and Disbelief—get no more time in your life. Starting today, you are figuratively tossing all those individuals listed above overboard. But first, because all people have value, I believe it would be prudent to have discussions with all those listed above. Prepare them for your newfound revelation and inform them that they are serving to block the vision you know is waiting to emerge. Each of these people can have access to you and give you counsel only if they lose the Jonah qualities that placed them on this list. You may be surprised that some on the list had no idea about the effects they were having and may find a way to unblock their own visions.

From this point forward, your vision will no longer be blocked by those who have a toxic effect on it. Now it is time to look for different people.

ESTABLISHING EMPOWERING RELATIONSHIPS

We all have a definite need to establish empowering relationships. When the right people come into your life, they bring insight, vision, passion, experience, wisdom, concern, and faith from which you can draw to move your vision forward. Now that you've eliminated or redirected those who were standing in opposition to your vision, how do you identify the right relationships? What kinds of people are we looking for to propel us to the next level—people who will empower us to succeed and conquer all that we desire?

I have been blessed to have three individuals—Saundra, Jack, and Mike—impact my life in a profound way. A short look at my relationship with each one will serve as an example for how to identify the characteristics of empowering relationships.

Let's take Saundra first. My relationship with Saundra is a very intimate one. I realize some might say, "She's your wife, so you have to say she empowers you." But the truth is that over the past fifteen years, Saundra and I have worked with enough troubled married couples that I realize just because someone is your spouse does not mean you share an empowering relationship—too many of these couples actually had destructive relationships. So I am blessed and thankful that my wife is also a strong empowering source. Saundra has unique gifts and qualities. She is the most calming, nurturing, and compassionate person I have ever met. She and I share a deep respect and love for one another that is unrivaled in my mind. The insight she delivers to some of life's most difficult situations always amazes me. She is on this list because of her constant belief in and encouragement for the things I attempt. Saundra is by far my greatest supporter and loudest cheerleader. No matter what circumstances I face, Saundra says, "You can do it, Babe." Those words never get old and they fuel my passion for life, for serving others and for helping humanity in any way I can. The words she speaks ring louder than a coach on the sidelines of a major sporting event. "You can do it" spoken by Saundra screams empowerment and encouragement for me to move to the finish line and win.

Jack is a dear friend with whom I have had the privilege of traveling and speaking at conferences. He is a great leader who has brought some very timely and needed humanitarian relief to areas of northern Iraq after devastating bombs blew apart villages there. Jack would describe himself as a "curmudgeon," but I don't think he really lives up to that description. Jack and I have been through some really interesting situations together, and the trauma of each one has only solidified our friendship. Jack is one of those people I can always count on for the truth. He is a great sounding board and offers responses that are always motivated with my best interest in mind. I believe Jack solely gives advice that considers his friends' future and success.

Mike and I met when I was a teller at a local credit union and he was hired as the new branch manager. He was retiring from banking and had decided to give credit union life a try. Not long after we met, Mike and I developed a deep appreciation for one another. Mike, being nearly thirty years my senior, offered invaluable wisdom and direction for an up-and-coming leader. Mike is a great cheerleader as well. But the main reason Mike is on this list is that he is extremely positive at every encounter. When you're going through your worst, he offers words of hope. When life seems overwhelming, he offers wisdom to make it through. Mike and I have known each other for over twenty years, and we have been there for each other through some of life's most tragic battles. My relationship with Mike has been and continues to be inspirational.

These three relationships have helped me determine the characteristics of the kinds of people with whom you want to have empowering relationships. When incredible people enter your life, learning how to hold on to the ones who empower you helps you to release your vision and conquer some of life's greatest challenges.

Empowering relationships should have the following characteristics:

1. **Be Built on Trust:** I know the three people I listed are in my corner no matter what. Our relationships have been proven by experiences that formed our trust and confidence in each other. That doesn't mean we don't make mistakes, but it means that even in our mistakes, we have the opportunities to learn, strengthen our relationship, and move beyond those errors.

2. **Have Your Best Interest In Mind:** You know an empowering relationship when the advice you receive motivates, encourages, and empowers you to conquer. It is driven by "what's best for you" instead of what's best for the other person. Remember that insecure people are challenged by your success and their advice will reflect that challenge. Empowered relationships are motivated by your success and your achievement, and the other person will serve as your sounding board and confidante in the midst of your battles.

3. **Positive Praise and Perspective:** We all need cheerleaders, champions, and coaches to get where we are going in life. People who are in empowering relationships with you will offer you positive feedback, praise for your successes, and valuable perspectives that look at alternatives to your objectives and obstacles.

4. **Mutually Beneficial:** In each of my empowering relationships, I have had the privilege of putting in as much as I have gotten out. I cherish each relationship and would move heaven and hell to help each person in his or her time of need. I invest in these relationships, not because of what I get out of them, but because of what they represent in my life. Empowering relationships should be mutually beneficial and provide you with great opportunities to serve. Over the years, our lives have gone through many situations, and each time, we have pulled for each other to make it through. Each of us serves the other and provides benefits to both of us.

5. **Unrelenting Belief:** One of the greatest testaments to an empowering relationship is the constant belief each person has in the other. No matter whether you are on top of the mountain or underneath it, the people in these relationships have an unrelenting belief that I am fully going to achieve my heart's desires and my life's calling. It is so incredible to know that even when I am doubting myself, there are people who never do.

These qualities are worth more than mounds of gold or the fattest bank account. I love Walter Winchell's quote "A friend is someone who walks in when others walk out." That describes who you are looking for to have a voice in your life—someone who will walk in when others are walking out. Someone who will believe in you, fight next to you, and help you unblock your vision so it flows rapidly.

Who in your life currently displays the qualities found in empowering relationships?

_____   _____

_____   _____

What qualities do you possess that make you the kind of person someone needs in his or her life?

_____   _____

_____   _____

_____   _____

For whom can you display these qualities?

_____   _____

_____   _____

_____   _____

ELEVATING YOUR VISION BY ELEVATING YOUR RELATIONSHIPS

No one climbs the ladder of success alone. Reaching your goals will require connection with many people along the way. You will need collaboration, encouragement, inspiration, and in some cases, direction. Whom you choose to associate with can determine the level of your overall success. Some people just seem to help you soar. They have the ability to see things from a wider angle or speak to you in a way that brings clarity and focus to a tough situation. They can open doors that would otherwise remain closed.

Jim Rohn says, "You are the average of the five people you spend the most time with, including yourself." What Jim is saying is that the relationships you keep have a profound effect on your life and on your thinking. An old English proverb says, "A man is known by the company he keeps." What kind of company are you keeping? There should be people in your life who push you beyond your own limitations and help you see things from a broader perspective. A distinct difference exists in the way successful people and average people think. The key to elevating your vision begins with putting some of these different thinkers in your life and learning to think the way they do.

From whom do you draw your inspiration? Whose advice and direction do you follow? Whom do you watch and emulate in your life? Those people are special and should be the ones with whom you try to spend the majority of your time.

This group should include:

1. **Successful People on the Move and Making a Difference:** Every community has a group of people doing great things and accomplishing great work for that community or for their businesses. These people have a contagious "can do" spirit, and they

think differently than average people. For instance, successful people have an action mentality; they dream big, think logically rather than emotionally about money, follow their passions, and they teach their children how to succeed. There are countless other ways successful people think differently than average people. To benefit from those differences, you need to associate with this group of people. Truly successful people will want to see you succeed as well. That sort of guilt by association will begin to work on you so you find yourself thinking differently, aiming higher, and seeing things from a very different perspective—one of success. Once you begin to release your vision and make it a reality, successful people will help push you to the finish line.

I have found in my own life that successful people provide a great motivation to keep me moving and accomplishing more. For example, I am an avid golfer, although not a great one. I like to play as much as possible during the summer months in the Pacific Northwest. As a business professional, I have the opportunity to play golf on a more regular basis with clients, and in charity tournaments and at other worthwhile events. It is always fun to get outside, hit a ball around the course, and try to beat my best score. I have a few clients who are very low handicap golfers and play on a very regular basis; it is always great to get on the course with them and learn from them. I am not ashamed that they usually (okay, always) beat me because I learn so much just from being on the course with them, including course management, how they strike the ball, proper stance, swing speed, club head placement, foot placement, teeing the ball properly, and of course, etiquette. I am constantly watching and picking up secrets and tools they use to play the game well. Whether I become a low handicap golfer or not is really not the point; I get better every time I get the opportunity to play.

In business, the same is true. I have the best time and accomplish the most in my career and business when I am associated with successful people. I frequently attend social or business-related functions where I find myself engaged in conversation with certain men and women of influence in my community. I look to them for friendship and brainstorming as I approach various business decisions and objectives. I am usually the first one at these functions, and I am typically the last to leave. The reason is simple: as a business professional, I am always on the lookout for the edge—that bit of knowledge, wisdom, or experience that can propel me into my destiny. Successful people have that edge. They have been through some battles and tell their war stories every chance they get. My goal is to get in close enough proximity to engage them in direct conversation so I can hear what they have to say. Like when I am on the golf course, I am watching and listening for the cues and clues to their success—the values and skills I can implement in my own life and business that will propel me into my future.

2. **Networking Connections:** How many times have you been to a networking event only to leave disappointed? In every community, dozens of groups or clubs get together with the solitary goal of referring business to each other. These groups can be phenomenal sources of business and relationships that can carry your vision into reality. An old adage says, "People do business with friends, so to do more business, make more friends". That is exactly what networking groups are about. Meeting new people and making new friends.

As a salesperson, I have been to hundreds of events, leads groups, sales clubs, social nights, themed networking, and many others.

I really like networking because there are typically 35-100 people gathered in a room who are passionate about what they do and where they are going, and they want to share their experiences with you. However, when I first began attending these events, I would leave frustrated because I wasn't really gaining any business from them. After a couple of years, I realized I was approaching networking completely wrong. I had thought these events were intended for selling each other your latest greatest product when, in fact, I was simply there to meet people and develop new relationships.

Today, networking has taken on a completely different tone for my business. I go to each event with the sole focus of collecting five business cards from people with whom I have had a meaningful conversation. I am not looking to sell them anything; in fact, I mainly ask questions and get to know who they are and what they do. I can usually tell from the conversation whether I want to get to know a person better.

What happens after the event is what provides the punch and power in the process. Within the next two weeks, I try to schedule lunch or coffee with each of the people I met. At the lunch or coffee, I continue to maintain the perspective that I want to get to know the person and his or her business even better. I'm still not trying to sell anything. What I am looking for are connection points—ways to refer business to my newfound friend, to develop a longer lasting relationship, and to add that person to my circle of friends.

As you develop your vision and begin to implement your plans, many of the people you network with will become cheerleaders and supporters for your new endeavors. Remember, many of these people are up-and-coming entrepreneurs who are excited about sharing their visions with you, and when you support them in their visions, they will want to return the favor.

You can find networking opportunities in nearly every community. Local chambers of commerce, economic development organizations, LeTip International, or sometimes, your local business association can provide a list of local networking groups or events.

3. **People Who Are Where You Want to Be:** When you are developing your vision and it begins to materialize, it is always healthy to find people who have been where you want to be. Throughout my business career and professional life, I have made it a practice to find people who are doing the kinds of things I want to do and to "look through their eyes." By that, I mean I try to spend time with them and ask questions about what they are looking for, how they assess situations, why they make certain decisions, and why they employ certain strategies.

   When I was a branch manager in a large national bank, I had been very successful, so I dreamt of being promoted to district manager. This promotion would put me in the executive level of management, and I would be commanding a territory of managers and multiple lines of business from lending to investments. I could see myself in that position, and I believed I had the training, experience, and skills required. Before making the push to reach that level, I reached out to the current district manager to take him to coffee or lunch on a semi-regular basis. During these sessions, I was clearly focused on my interview questions and learning as much as possible about his processes, procedures, decisions, leadership style, and philosophies for doing business. My total objective was to see things through his eyes.

Once I stepped into the role of district manager, it was like I had been working the job for many months. My experience through my district manager served me exponentially in the new role. I quickly began motivating my team, casting vision, and making decisions to move our group to the top of the company in short order, seeing everything from a senior district manager's perspective. Of course, I did things Eric-style, but I know I dodged a few bullets and missed a few land mines because of the knowledge I had gleaned from those meetings.

Looking through others' wise and experienced eyes is a valuable tool. If you have a teachable spirit and can slow down long enough to hear what others have to say and see things from their perspectives, you can save yourself much heartache and headache as you begin to launch your vision into reality.

SURROUNDING YOURSELF WITH SUCCESS

This chapter would not be complete if we didn't talk about the kind of people who should surround you. Earlier, we discussed the value people bring no matter who they are or what they do. We uncovered the Jonahs in your life who should be "tossed overboard." We also addressed empowering relationships and elevating your relationships. But there is also a group of people who should be close to you—an inner circle if you will. People who can be trusted with ideas, collaboration, coaching, and sometimes handing you the truth.

This group includes:

1. **Mentors:** Men and women who agree to mentor an up-and-coming professional are priceless. Unlike coaches, they are not typically paid for their services; mentors agree to help you out of the goodness of their hearts and the satisfaction of seeing

you succeed. I have had the privilege of calling several people mentors in my life. One of the great ones is Mike. During the years I was a teller at a local credit union, I also was going to college at night on my way to law school. I had my eyes set on getting a degree in corporate law and grand plans of handling corporate mergers and acquisitions. After the first year, I decided to change my major to business and continue my career in the banking industry. I was loving what I was doing and could see a great future in banking for me. Mike had accomplished so many things in his career from retail branch management to commercial lender and really everything in between. His last role before coming to the credit union was in senior management of a savings and loan. I asked Mike to be my mentor and guide me up the ladder of success in the banking profession. His advice has been invaluable. At each rung, I could call him to discuss the challenges and successes I was experiencing. He could quickly cut to the core of problematic situations and guide me to quick resolutions. One quality he instilled in me lives on today. Mike taught me "We are not in the banking business; we are in the people business. The people we encounter have dreams, and we help make those dreams come true." I have lived by that mantra in every aspect of my life. No matter what I am doing, whether it be senior pastor at a church or senior executive at a bank, I am always in the people business, looking to help people make their dreams come true.

Mentors are great because they can help sharpen you, help you to pull true, and help you to stay the course. Mentors are everywhere. Countless individuals are eager to share their knowledge and experiences with you. Mentors are typically just waiting to be asked. Most won't approach you and ask to be your mentor. Rarely is there a mentor sign-up sheet; it requires action on your part by having the courage to ask.

2. **Coaches—Business and Personal:** How do you get more done in less time more effectively? I continually contemplate that question. The answer is through coaching. This book has been a project inside of me for the past three years. I was inspired to write, compelled to create, but not motivated to start, and I was confused about the path. Hiring a coach to get this process to completion saved years of frustration and thousands of dollars of wasted expense. Throughout the years, I have had many coaches from academics to sports to business. Coaches play an integral part in sharpening your skills and giving you powerful techniques to cut through the piles of distractions and minutia. Again, the difference between a coach and a mentor is that a coach is paid, but he or she is dedicated to your success and helping you get to the top.

Top business leaders engage coaches to take them further in their careers and businesses. Coaches serve to keep you focused on the main thing without becoming distracted by the minor things. They help you make strategic decisions with precision and accuracy, saving you thousands of dollars compared to if you had made bad ones.

One of my favorite coaches was Coach King, my high school wrestling coach. He was always so encouraging and driven to see each of his wrestlers succeed. He taught me one thing in particular that I have carried throughout my life. He would say, "Scroggins, leave it all on the mat." He meant that at the end of each match, I should have nothing left, no moves I didn't try, no energy I didn't expend, and no passion I didn't deliver. Throughout my life, I have taken on many assignments, projects, and business ventures, and with each one, I leave it all on the mat. For example, each time I am asked to speak at a conference, church, or organization, I always attempt to deliver with passion, motivation, and inspiration, "leaving it all on the mat." My goal is to leave the audience members awestruck by what they heard and challenged to make changes in their lives. Without a coach, I would not have learned this valuable principle. Coaches help with leadership challenges and business strategy decisions.

The power of having a coach can transform your income earning potential and propel your growth exponentially. Eric Schmidt, CEO of Google, says, "Everyone needs a coach; coaches ask the questions no one else is asking, causing you to think through decisions very carefully."

3. **Pastors:** The value of a pastor is beyond monetary measurement. A pastor is someone who has spiritual care over a number of persons. As you grow your business, launch your vision, and begin to execute on your dream, often morality can become blurred and out of focus. A valued inner circle team member should be a pastor who can bring a reality check to the spiritual side of life. I spent six years as a senior pastor over a growing congregation with a large proportion of my congregation being business owners, company leaders, and some top level employees. During this time, I was able to be a spiritual sounding board for decisions, a great ear that would listen to the stresses of business ownership, and a voice of reason in times of chaos.

Pastors may or may not have a business background, but each spiritual advisor brings a deep understanding of life and spirit that can help guide you on your path to greatness. Some of the most enriching discussions I have had were with my pastor. Freely pouring out my soul over the confusing and frustrating situations I experience with someone who can provide a spiritual perspective has been a rich blessing; it has allowed me to find a tangible reality in what were otherwise overwhelming choices. Pastors can help reduce the stress you are carrying by offering solutions not typically in business manuals and educational textbooks. Their perspectives help you realize the greater purpose you have and the future you hold.

SUMMARY

People are the most important aspect of life. Relationships you build can assist you in moving from place to place and level to level as you make your vision a reality. Some people can actually fit the bill as vision blockers who cause you to lose sight of the bigger picture and keep you from realizing your dream.

The Jonahs in your life who cause storms to rage and the seas to roar can cost you years of progress and mounds of heartache. Admitting these people on your ship of life can be fatal for your dream. Toss them overboard and move on to people who are waiting to push you to the next level. Mentors, coaches, pastors, and relationships that empower you to succeed and celebrate your successes should be the highest of priorities.

Be on the lookout for those special people who serve a very real and distinct purpose in removing the vision blockers and releasing your dream. Connecting correctly is the key.

PART TWO

Moving Toward Your Destiny

CHAPTER 10

Making Lasting Change

"Your life does not get better by chance; it gets better by change."
— Jim Rohn

What now? Over the past several chapters, you have identified some emotional, physical, and personal characteristics that may have been standing in your way, and you received suggestions for removing them from your life. If it's true that knowledge is king, then you are reigning royalty, ready to rule over your vision forever.

My hope is that by reading this book, you recognize what has been stopping you from moving forward, blocking your vision, and keeping you from dreaming about the future you were designed to own. Potentially, you have gained revelation and inspiration, and you have acquired a sense of perspective regarding the barrier keeping you where you are today.

Over the years, as I have worked with countless individuals and couples to improve their lives, businesses, relationships, and decision-making skills, one thing has become abundantly clear for me:

Change is not easy! But as the old proverb says, "Nothing worth having comes easy." The tendency is to read a book like this, hear a great motivational speaker or a sermon at church, and be overwhelmed with excitement to change—but then busyness, life, and responsibilities creep in and steal the zeal. Change won't happen if the initial spark of inspiration never catches fire to burn inside you. In speaking to audiences, churches, and business groups, my focus has always been to present the challenges alongside the potential solutions for instilling lifelong change. I have never desired to be just the spark, but to continue to fan the flame of change.

The truth, however, is that change is only possible if you do it! It only happens when are willing to put in the work, execute the plan, and commit to making change. Over the next several pages, you will explore insights and strategies for making lasting change. I challenge you to read and execute them. Take a risk and watch change happen.

DISCOVERING THE NEED TO CHANGE

How honest can you be with you? As you look at the landscape of your life, are you accomplishing all you hoped to accomplish? Do you possess the resources you hoped to possess? Are you earning at the level you hoped to earn? Is your business, ministry, or non-profit reaching as far or making as great an impact as you hoped it would? If you answered "No" to any of these questions, then something is not right. So often we shift the blame for the "no" responses to other people or catastrophic situations, but frequently, the reason you are not achieving, impacting, growing, or building is YOU! Zig Ziglar said, "People want attention to go with their problems; they want solutions to fix the problem, answers for them, and someone else to handle them. When you point out the actual problem, they get offended." He went on to say, "People who are the problem never realize it."

Realizing you need to change is really the first step in the right direction. As you've been reading this book, you've probably had some "ah ha" moments when you've realized, "Yes, that's me; I do that," and then asked, "How do I stop doing that?" Congratulations! That's the first step to success—recognition.

Whether you have identified a destructive habit or a personal trait that needs changing, the fact that you have recognized the issue allows you to take personal action to correct the behavior. This personal self-discovery can be frightening. It causes some people to ask, "What is wrong with me?" and "Why is this happening to me?" and even "Why do I do that? Am I damaged?" The answer is simply that you are a human living the life of a human who is being human. Your experiences, your culture, and your life have led you right to where you are. Now it's time to redirect those elements into positive, focused change that will take you to your vision.

Realize, first, you are not alone. Every one of us has something in his or her life that needs to change. Something that needs to be improved, addressed, changed, corrected, or eliminated. EVERYONE! Without exception, each one of us can improve and be better. The difference between truly great people and those who don't accomplish much is that great people recognize the need to change and take action to do it. Their desire to be great outweighs their desire to stay the same. Their desire to be great outweighs their fear of changing. Their egos are not so fragile that they don't try to change.

The people accomplishing great things realize that change is not a threat to their value; it's just a threat to their thinking and, ultimately, their behaviors.

Take the time to do some self-examination. Put together a self-assessment to review your current situation, your current thinking, and your current behaviors. What one thing do you want to change? What needs to change in your life that will unblock the vision and release your destiny?

Take a look at your life. What is keeping you from reaching your goal, achieving your destiny, or seeing your vision? Write it down.

_____

_____

What changes are needed to remove the vision blocker?

_____

_____

Do you recognize that the change needs to be in you?

_____

Are you willing to do what it takes to make the change?

_____

MAKING THE DECISION TO CHANGE

Seems like a relatively simple concept: To make change, I have to decide to change. The problem is that most people are inspired to change, but they don't decide to change. They feel a compulsion to change, but they don't make the decision. They promise to change, but they don't decide to do it. To make lasting change in your life, you must *decide*.

The dictionary defines decide as "to solve or conclude by giving victory to one side." A decision gives the changed behavior victory over the previous behavior. By making your new behavior the victor, not the victim, you begin to unleash tremendous power in your life. But you have to make the decision.

I have counseled people over the years who believed it was a good idea to make a change. They heard the concepts and thought, "Wow, that is a great idea; I should put that in practice in my own life," but they failed to make the decision to give victory to this new idea.

The decision to change comes when something deep within you realizes that to stay the same does not get you to your goal. It doesn't allow you to reach your vision or dream. Deciding to change is a shifting deep within you that says, "I am letting go of the past and pursuing the future with passion and aggression."

The Apostle Paul said it this way in Philippians 3:13, "This one thing I do, forgetting the things in my past and pursuing the things which are ahead." Paul made the decision that what was in his past was past and that his future was where he needed to go.

To make lasting change, you are not making the promise to change; you are making the decision to change. A promise is an expression of what may be expected, but it is not a commitment for what will be expected. You hear story after story of broken promises, missed dreams, and bad behaviors that continue. How many times have you made the promise to start working out, eat better, stop causing chaos, treat your spouse better, or be a better employee? If you are like most of us, every year you make a New Year's resolution to make some grand change, only to find you probably don't make it to the end of January and the old habits are back. Why is that? It's because you made the promise or resolution, but you never made the decision. Your desire to stay the same outweighed your desire to change. It isn't until you declare victory for the change that change will take place.

Something special happens when you make an unbridled, deep-seated, and passionate decision to change. It becomes an irrevocable and unforgettable commitment. The decision to change goes beyond your emotion, beyond your reasoning, beyond your intellectual understanding to a place deep within your soul that causes you to take action.

I can remember being a shy high school student. The abuse from my upbringing was still playing a major role in my life and decisions. As a junior, I was that kid no one really knew. Shy and scared, I really didn't make many friends. Absolutely none who were female. A couple of guys in the neighborhood I could classify as friends. But overall, I was afraid to engage new people in conversation and would not approach girls at any cost. One girl in the neighborhood befriended me, but again, my shyness got the best of me. One November afternoon after school, I remember sitting in my parents' basement, feeling frustration, fear, and isolation. I was miserable, afraid to approach anyone new, and consequently, missing out on high school experiences I should have enjoyed and long remembered. Frustrated with being so alone and afraid, I couldn't take it anymore, so that day, I became determined to change my circumstances. I decided that the next day at school, I would find the most popular person I could and engage him or her in conversation. I would conquer my fear and actually talk to someone in "that" group. So the next day, having worked up my courage, sweaty palms and all, I approached Kim and engaged her in conversation. My opening line could have used some work, but nonetheless, I started talking to her. To my surprise, she talked back. We had a great conversation, and eventually, Kim became my first date.

That experience taught me that no matter what needs to be changed in my life, it starts with a decision. Without the decision, nothing will be accomplished. I was driven not to live a life of fear or one without friends—girlfriends in particular. I now wanted to live life to the fullest. Once the decision settled deep inside me, nothing was going to cause me not to change.

The decision is yours. No one can make it for you. It is all up to you. Anything short of making that decision will leave you frustrated and in the same place you are today. If you don't make the decision, you leave yourself open to excuses and circumstances that can keep you from making lasting change.

Think about the last time you tried to make a change—maybe it was starting a new work-out program, changing your eating habits, quitting a bad habit, or starting a business. Whatever it was, what caused this change not to last?

_____

_____

_____

CREATING A PLAN FOR CHANGE

Now that you've made the decision to change, it's time to create and implement a plan. The planning process takes your decision, assigns action items and a strategy to ensure your decision is executed, and makes the decision last. Your success depends on a well-thought-out, well-executed plan to change. Benjamin Franklin said, "If you fail to plan, you are planning to fail." What are the components to a plan that will help ensure your success?

The truth is that plans may vary between individuals. Yours may not look like mine or anyone else's, but the concept of having a plan should not vary. A well-constructed plan for change should contain three key elements:

1. **Clarity:** Your changed thinking, changed behaviors, and changed habits should be clear and concise. You should be able to communicate with the utmost clarity what you are going to do and how you are going to accomplish the change. Too often, the expectations to change are so vague that accomplishing them is difficult. Be clear and know what change you want to make. Write it down or repeat it to yourself so you're clear about it. For example: "I no longer smoke cigarettes." "My life is free of strife." "I am focused in my mind, know the direction I am headed, and am not double-minded." "I am free from this pain; I am free and powerful over my past."

2. **Commitment:** A well-constructed plan contains the commitment that emulates the decision you have already made. Statements like "I will" instead of "I should" or "I will try" should be predominant throughout the plan. Remember, you have already made the decision to make this change, so trying shouldn't be the concern; doing should. It's like Yoda said, "Do or do not. There is no try."

3. **Consistency:** In order to make lasting change, you have to replace previous behaviors with new ones that reflect the change. The plan should contain activities or situations that allow you to act on your new changed behavior or thought processes. This consistency will begin to solidify the decisions you have made.

My rudimentary plan to meet new people and break out of my shell contained three very distinct parts: 1) Decide, 2) Plan, 3) Act. This same plan has the building blocks for making permanent change in your own life. We already discussed the decision; now let's discuss the plan, and finally, we will discuss the action.

Planning and action are very closely aligned. Whatever you plan to do must have an associated action step in order to solidify the behavior and have it become part of your nature. This can be very simple and straightforward. Such as:

Plan	Action
I will talk to the most popular person I can find	Talk to Kim
I will work out three days a week for one hour	Mon, Wed, Fri schedule time at gym and then go
I will stop belittling my wife	Choose uplifting statements to say to her; then say them
I will stop smoking	Don't buy cigarettes; instead, buy and eat fruit
I will eat healthily	Buy healthy food; don't buy junk food. Find healthy recipes and make healthy meals
I will make more money	Find a new job, start my business, write my book…

Whatever the change happens to be, nothing will be done without a decision, a plan to execute on the decision, and finally, taking formal action.

The action is where "the rubber meets the road." If you decide to lose weight, create a plan for weight loss, and then never do anything in the plan, you won't hit the target or reach the goal. Confucius said, "When it's obvious that the goals cannot be reached, don't adjust the goals; adjust the action." I also love Dale Carnegie's quote, "Inaction breeds doubt and fear. Action breeds confidence and courage. If you want to conquer fear, do not sit home and think about it. Go out and get busy."

That sums it up. Action breeds courage and confidence. Taking action to make your change gives you the courage and confidence to continue.

In high school, the action I took was approaching Kim and engaging her in a wonderful, albeit short conversation. She was very kind to continue the conversation with me. This action gave me the confidence to ask her out on a date; then I gained the confidence to speak to other people, which ultimately resulted in my being named "the most spirited" of our senior class. The courage and confidence that I built speaking to Kim grew to where I now have the confidence to speak before thousands of people at conferences around the world.

What started as a decision to make a change, resulted in a plan that ultimately became action. That process has taken me to wonderful levels of success and a willingness to talk to anyone, anywhere.

Change Plan Worksheet

Decide:

What change do I want to make?

Why is this change important to my life?

Plan:

What are the steps I need to take to make this change?

1.

2.

3.

4.

Who are the people who can help me?

Act:

What steps will I take to implement the plan?

1.

2.

3.

4.

I will know the plan is working if:

What are some things that could deter my change?

How will I change course if the plan isn't working?

ENLISTING SUPPORT

One area where you might struggle when trying to make change is if you attempt to go it alone. While making change is your decision and totally up to you, it doesn't mean you have to make the trip by yourself. A great way to help ensure your success is to enlist supporters who are assigned the responsibilities of accountability partners, trusted advisors, and cheerleaders. Change is hard to make when you believe you are the only one facing the challenge; no one recognizes your accomplishments, and you don't have anyone with whom to talk or strategize.

Three people should be enlisted to join your battle for change:

1. **Accountability Partner:** A good accountability partner's value is without measure. Whom you choose for this role is very important. First, let me state that family members make very poor choices for accountability partners. They are too emotionally tied to you and are often concerned with not offending you. Their love and appreciation for you trumps their objectivity to get you to the goal. Family members can be a great support—just not in the role of accountability. In order to have an effective accountability partner, you must be willing to be honest and trusting with this person. An accountability partner is someone to whom you give the exclusive responsibility of holding you accountable for the daily decisions you make and the things you do. The person must possess the strength to ask you very difficult questions without being offended by your answers or upset by your responses. Your accountability partner should be someone who challenges you to change and is not afraid to ask the very difficult questions. This person is truly invested in your success and can help you focus on your own personal decision to change. Proverbs 27:17 says, "Iron sharpens iron, and one man sharpens another." An account-

ability partner will have this goal to help you sharpen yourself and more accurately and swiftly make the change.

2. **Trusted Advisor:** When making a change, you will be faced with many decisions that require strategy, focus, experience, and wisdom to navigate successfully. A trusted advisor can offer objectivity to make great decisions and also double as a willing ear to unload the stresses of the change. Selecting the right trusted advisor requires some forethought. In the business community, trusted advisors serve as consultants and confidantes as you make decisions to grow your business. In your personal life, this person could be a pastor, community leader, or other person you can trust and confide in. It should be someone who can help you navigate through the confusing emotions that will drive your decisions in the change process.

   Trusted advisors can give you timely and relevant information to make the best decisions, provide you with suggestions that you wouldn't normally think about, and bring a sense of objectivity to your life and goals. This monumental person or group of people allows you to make change more swiftly. Having someone you can share your heart with will allow you the freedom to make the change and reinforce that you are not doing this alone.

3. **Cheerleaders:** Cheerleading first emerged in the late 1800s during a losing streak for the University of Minnesota's football team. Johnny Campbell assembled a crowd of people, picked up a megaphone, and began to cheer the team to a victorious season, which birthed the modern day cheer. What the team couldn't accomplish on its own, Johnny and his assembled crowd of excited, exuberant, and enthusiastic cheer participants did together. The cheers gave the team encouragement and a sense of passion, despite their losing streak. Knowing

they had support on the sidelines encouraged the team members and helped change their thinking, their perspective, and their vision, and so, they were cheered on to victory!

Everyone needs the encouraging and passionate praise of a cheerleader or a positive voice cheering him on from the sidelines—someone who will rally the troops and cheer for you no matter what is happening, or where you are in the battle. A cheerleader sees you as victoriously winning the battle and will scream at the top of his or her lungs while you push forward to victory.

Enlisting a cheerleader may require some action on your part. Some people in your life naturally migrate to cheering you on. You can identify those individuals by their solid belief in you, but you may need to be specific about what you're looking for from them. A simple explanation that says, "I am about to make some major change in my life and I would really appreciate hearing your words of encouragement through the process" can go a long way toward enlisting a supporter and cheerleader.

I personally have had several cheerleaders in my life. My wife is a great supporter. She typically travels with me to speaking engagements, is by my side every time I try to conquer anything, and always tells me, "You can do it, Babe." Several others have offered me that timely, encouraging word of affirmation that propelled me to the next level of success.

Who in your life can serve in these three roles? If you can find more than one for each role, all the better.

Accountability Partner

_____

_____

Trusted Advisor

_____

_____

Cheerleader

_____

_____

TELLING THE STORY

What are you telling others and yourself about your change? Do you continue to identify yourself as the pre-change you, or do you declare the changes made in your life? So much of what we are is what we tell ourselves we are. What is your testimony for how you overcame the test? My testimony is a declaration to others that I passed with flying colors; it is a celebration of how I was able to overcome.

When I tell the story of my change, it further confirms my change in my heart, in my head, and ultimately, in my actions. My words begin to write upon my heart what I hope to achieve. Telling the story allows my words to lead me to the change I seek.

The famous actor, Jim Carrey, tells the story of how when he was struggling to find acting jobs and living very poorly, he went to the top of a peak, looked over Los Angeles, and began to dream. It was at that moment that he wrote himself a check for $10 million. In the memo line, he wrote "for acting services rendered." In effect, he was professing that someday he would be able to cash a $10 million check for acting. Today, Jim Carrey commands more that $10 million for the films in which he stars.

Tell your story! Write it down and tell it to everyone you know and don't know. Your story is powerful. I overcame _____ by doing _____! You can't imagine how therapeutic the telling of the story will become. You will begin to change your own thinking when you begin to change how you talk about the things you are doing.

I realize this idea can sound ridiculous, but just test the theory. Start telling the story about your new changed life today. Watch others' reactions and also how your own thoughts change to line up with the story you are telling.

Just like in the planning section, you say "I will _____," in this section you should be saying, "I am _____" to declare the change in your life. Job 22:28 says, "Declare a thing and it will be established for you."

Make your declaration, tell your story, and begin to be the person you are talking about.

Write down your story right now. What change have you made and what have you become?

_____

_____

_____

_____

_____

_____

_____

SUMMARY

It's true that change is not easy and you are the only one who can make it. To make real lasting change, you must decide that the change is necessary, make a plan to make the change, and then take action on the plan. I believe that no challenge is too difficult for you to overcome and no change is too great for you to accomplish.

The change discussed in this book has great rewards. It allows you to remove the obstacles to your destiny and lets your vision become a reality. Enlisting the support of your accountability partners, trusted advisors, and cheerleaders helps you to reach the finish line without the agony of defeat.

I believe you can do it! Make the lasting change now.

CHAPTER 11

Discovering Your Moral Authority

"The son can do nothing by himself, only what he sees the Father do."

— Jesus

Every one of us is driven by something. We see, we hear, and we do. That is the order for accomplishing great things. The question is: Where are we looking and what are we hearing? In the last chapter, we discussed making lasting change, and I conveyed some concepts that will help you make those changes and make them last. The concepts written there will allow you to conquer whatever change is put before you.

In this chapter, we will discuss a key element that grounds every great leader and drives each one to greatness: a moral authority. This authority becomes the basis for moral conviction, the supreme accountability partner who is concerned with eternal consequence more than earthly reputation. In my life, that supreme account-ability partner is God, or more specifically, Jesus Christ.

Having a moral authority, a Higher Power, someone who is looking out and looking ahead, brings real comfort and indescribable peace as you experience the challenges of life's journey. This chapter will describe that relationship and what leads to discovering your own moral authority.

DOING WHATEVER FEELS RIGHT IS WRONG

How do we make decisions regarding what's right and wrong? Where do we find the ideal to be honest? How do we know which path is right and which is wrong? And where do we go from here? I mean after this life, what happens? All of these questions and more have answers, real answers.

So often in business, our personal life, our relationships, and raising our kids, we are faced with difficult decisions and having to choose the correct path. Life can seem overwhelming, especially when it is driven by doing whatever we decide is right in the moment. Too often, when I do whatever feels right, it actually leads me wrong.

Throughout my adult life, I have been guided by a set of moral principles outlined in the Bible. Reading those pages has become a part of my everyday life. The decision to include this practice in my life has added value and brought answers to previously unanswered questions. The best-selling book of all time is written to speak to every life, everywhere, and to provide solid answers to the toughest questions.

I titled this section "Doing Whatever Feels Right is Wrong" because those words describe exactly what I used to do. I was guided by an internal morality based on my own good judgment and upbringing (which I already revealed was not that great). I lived my life making the most of my own morality, not really hurting anyone, living as a law-abiding citizen, and yet I was completely wrong. Wrong because those decisions were leaving me feeling empty, misguided, and unfocused.

While I was doing what I thought was right, I was not doing anything to satisfy what was most crying out for attention: my heart.

Then I realized that morality is a real thing! Real, but not something based on my opinion or personal construct; it is based on a time-tested and eternal set of principles. Those principles, outlined in Scripture, allow us to lead a happy, productive, eternity-bound life. A life I look forward to every day.

The age old questions are: "What happens to us after this life?" "Who has the ultimate authority in life?" and "Does God exist?" My search for the answers to these questions led me to my relationship with Jesus Christ. I realized that for me, doing whatever feels right was very wrong, so I chose to do what Christ says is right.

When I came to realize that everything I create here on earth has a temporal value, I knew the only true pursuit is one that has eternal consequence. As a result, I accepted Jesus Christ as my personal Lord and Savior in February, 1993. Since then, my life has gained strength, excitement, passion, and direction, and Jesus Christ has guided, protected, and blessed me every step of the way. He has shown me new and better ways to live life to help others do the same.

LISTENING TO HIS ANSWER

So many of life's questions need answers. Where do you turn for the kind of answer that can speak directly to your situation? I believe the answers to life's big questions are found within the pages of the Bible. This amazing and timeless book has brought wisdom to so many of life's great leaders. Generation after generation, people have turned to those pages to find counsel, wisdom, comfort, and direction. Our forefathers used its wisdom as they crafted our nation's founding documents. Many of these men could quote the Bible chapter and verse, gleaning steadfast answers from its pages for an ever-changing society.

I believe the Bible holds answers for you as well. I challenge you to check it out for yourself. Read through it, let the words leap from the pages of this amazing book, and hear the answers God would offer to some of your most difficult situations. I know in my life, through some of my craziest moments, I have been able to find comfort and answers as I read through each story.

TRUSTING HIS DIRECTION

To believe God is to know His heart and to understand that His desire for you is to be blessed. As you read the Bible, you will find that direction flows from its pages. A subtle nudge will lead you in a different direction. A still small voice will speak to you, giving you instruction—a voice that calls from your soul, asking for fellowship with you.

The key here is to trust that direction. So often, we profess that we believe in God as a moral authority; we even hear Him give us direction, but then we ignore it completely. The question that then comes to mind is: "Why believe if you are simply going to ignore?"

Jeremiah 29:11 says, "'I know the plans I have for you,' says the Lord, 'plans to prosper you and not to harm you, plans to give you a hope and a future.'" If we understand that He knows the plans He has already set for us, our only need is to find those plans, to hear Him and allow Him to guide us to the plan He established to give us hope and allow us to prosper.

Knowing that His direction for my life is to lead me to a plan of prosperity and hope is so exciting. It is awesome!

But can we trust? Are we continuing to doubt? What does it take to realize that all along, God through Jesus Christ has been searching for you?

BELIEVING

In Mark 5:36, Jesus says, "Don't be afraid, only believe." Belief can be a tough thing. In our "prove it to me," analytical, intellectually driven, information society, belief is tough because it requires something that can't be proven by spreadsheets, formulas, or equations. It requires faith—faith that there is someone greater than us, faith that there is a God, and faith that He sent a son—faith that His son was sent for you and me, sent to redeem this world and help us all to live life more abundantly. In fact, those are Jesus' actual words: "I came that you may have life and have it more abundantly" (John 10:10).

I challenge you to read the Bible with an open mind and an open heart. Take a leap of faith to believe the words written there and see whether they will in turn be written on your heart. Psalms 34:8 says, "Taste and see that the Lord is good. Blessed are those that trust in Him." I challenge you to take a taste for yourself and see whether the Lord is good.

What do you believe?

_____

_____

_____

Do you believe in God?

_____

_____

_____

If your answer is "No," write out the reasons why you have doubts. I would also encourage you to seek answers to your questions by reading the Bible with the guidance of a pastor.

SUMMARY

Coming to terms with your morality and gaining an understanding that there is a Higher Power, someone who is watching over and watching out for you, brings a deep sense of comfort. Strive to gain a perspective that right and wrong are real decisions and that doing what is right brings with it a sense of stability and can drive blessings into your life in a very tangible way.

The Bible is a time-tested set of instructions for navigating life, written by inspired men to give us the secrets to living life successfully. Within its pages are time-honored traditions, rich historic content, and moral principles that are beyond the limitations of humanity. In its pages, God brings us face-to-face with His plan for our life and how we can succeed by subscribing to His offer.

I challenge you as I close this chapter to read the Bible for yourself. Take time to explore its wisdom and apply its truths to the situations you encounter. You might be surprised by what you discover.

CHAPTER 12

Leading with Vision

"Leadership is the capacity to translate vision into reality."
— Warren Bennis

Over the past several chapters, we have discussed overcoming various vision blockers. You have been on a journey to discover what could be stopping you from seeing your life's vision and dreams. As I stated in the opening chapter, vision is imperative for determining life's direction, purpose, and ultimately, the fulfillment you seek. Vision is vital! Proverbs 29:18 says, "Without vision, the people perish." The verse does not literally mean that people will die. You will remember that the word perish is translated "revolt, dissipate, or become unbridled." There is a distinct unsettling to living without vision. Life needs meaning, and the meaning is expressed through the vision you have for your life. Vision gives you a focal point for your life and for making decisions. Furthermore, the ability to birth a vision lies in being able to remove contaminants, pollutants, and corrosive material from the heart. The pure heart is what drives the vision.

I hope by now you are fairly fired up and ready to take things to the next level. As a salesperson, I get so excited about breaking through barriers and positioning myself to conquer the next challenge. When working with a sales prospect, several obstacles may keep the person from doing business with you. I love removing each of those obstacles and positioning myself to close the deal. Hopefully, by now you have identified some of the obstacles to your own vision and gained some strategies for removing them. Once they are removed, you are positioned to let the vision become clear.

I believe that understanding the end purpose will allow more specificity as you begin to write your vision and bring it forward. Therefore, in this chapter, we are going to talk about leading with that vision.

John Maxwell says, "Everything rises and falls on leadership." He goes on to say that "Leadership is influence, nothing more and nothing less." Leadership is about executing on vision, and vision is about taking people, primarily yourself, on a journey.

Let's take that journey!

GAINING DIRECTION

Unfortunately, when we are born, we are not handed a compass and a map labeled "To find life's directions." While receiving that kind of direction would be really cool, it is very farfetched. Finding direction isn't as easy as some might think. It seems as though the more options there are, the more technology advances, the more new industries emerge, and the more old industries expand, the more confused, dismayed, and stuck people become. The possibilities for work, volunteering, and getting involved are overwhelming and endless. Now more than ever before, you can do whatever you want to do! So how do you know which direction to go?

First things first, you have to know what you want. Maybe you are one of the many people living an unfulfilled life—a life full of missed dreams and passions. Not knowing what you want leads to doing the wrong thing and following the wrong path. Now that you have taken time to remove one or more of the vision blockers, spend some time thinking, really getting down to the place where you can meditate, pray, or focus. Ask yourself that very question: "What do I want out of this life?" Also ask yourself, "How do I want to be remembered?"

I love the story of Chris Gardner, portrayed by Will Smith in the film *The Pursuit of Happyness*. Chris finds himself homeless; his wife has left and he is the sole caretaker of his son. He is living in conditions that are unimaginable for many of us, bouncing from shelter to shelter, finding rest wherever he can, and trying to sell medical devices to get enough cash to eat and have a clean, dry bed. Chris is truly at the end of his everything when he meets a stockbroker who is living the life Chris has always dreamed of having, but until now, he has been doing all of the wrong things to get it. Chris enters an internship program at the brokerage firm to become a stockbroker. After his training is completed, Chris becomes the top salesperson and incredibly changes his circumstances forever. Because he went for it, he completely turned his life around.

So you might say, "What did Chris want?" Chris wanted to be off the streets, provide for his family, and live the life of someone wealthy. By watching the film, you realize that once he came to the conclusion that he could make those things happen and he focused on what he wanted, nothing could stop him.

What do you want? Really! Ask yourself that question free of other people's opinions, free from biased input, free from others' rationale. What do you want?

What do you want?

_____

_____

_____

To answer the question, you may need to spend some time under-standing your passions. Finding your passions can be a bit elusive. Things you do well may not necessarily be your passion. A passion is a powerful or compelling emotion or feeling toward something or someone. When you are passionate about something, your in-tensity rises, your focus narrows, your heart begins to beat faster, and every thought is consumed with thinking about the nucleus of your passion. Nineteenth century English author William Hazlitt said, "A strong passion for any object will ensure success, for the desire of the end will point out the means."

I want to provide some caution regarding the questions you are about to answer. Do not—I repeat, do not—allow your mind to analyze these things. Passion does not live in the mind; it lives in the heart, and therefore, the heart needs to be asked the questions. Your heart will give you the answers to the questions and will begin to reveal your passion. Remember, "Blessed are the pure in heart for they shall see…." The heart, free of contamination, will reveal its passion.

To find your passion, you need to ask yourself some serious ques-tions and be honest with yourself:

1. What are you good at? In what activity, skill, hobby, job, or task do you excel?

_____

2. What do you wish you could spend more of your time doing?

_____

3. What do you read about?

_____

4. What do you find yourself thinking about all the time?

_____

5. When you dream, what do you dream about?

_____

6. What gets you extremely excited?

_____

7. If you had to spend the rest of your life doing something without a vacation or time off, what would you do?

_____

8. What is happening in the world that absolutely fires you up?

_____

Finally, to find your direction, you "gotta go with your gifting," by which I mean the talents or areas where God has given you gifts. For example, I spent six years as senior pastor of a growing church. While this time was extremely rewarding and provided me with valuable experiences, it was not the most impactful period in my life. I can preach, I can teach, I can lead others spiritually, but my true gifting is in business, leadership, professional speaking, and helping people reach their dreams. Fortunately, those are my overwhelming passions as well. Once I shifted gears and operated in my gifting, things began to happen that I couldn't explain. Success began to find me and I started making impacts on multiple levels.

Going with your gifting is essential to determining your direction. So the next logical question is: "What is my gifting?" A number of tests can help you determine your gifting, such as the Myers-Briggs personality test, or the DISC profile. One of my favorite tests that does a thorough job of drilling down to the details is the StrengthsFinder exam in Tom Rath's book *StrengthsFinders*. The results will reflect your top five strengths and how those strengths translate into activities, behaviors, and tasks that you tend to love.

To lead with vision, you have to know what you want, understand your passion, and identify your gifting. By gaining a clear understanding of who you are and what you want, you are ready to take others with you on the journey.

TAKING OTHERS ALONG

Leadership has many definitions, including: the ability to cause others to go forward; taking command of a group; the position one assumes to lead an organization or group of people; or the act or office that moves people. Finally, there is John Maxwell's definition, "Leadership is influence, nothing more, nothing less." He asserts that leadership is the ability to influence individuals or groups to move in a direction. No matter which definition you choose, leadership is about people. An old proverb says, "If you think you are leading and no one is following, then you are just taking a walk." Leadership is always about people.

Leading with vision is exactly the same way. Once you decide what the passion is that's driving you and what you want by using your gifting, you will notice it all has to do with taking someone with you on your journey or impacting that person right where he or she is.

Your personal reason for having your vision and executing your dream may be to forward your career, live financially free, change the world, or free it from some horrendous atrocity, but none of those goals can be accomplished without impacting others' lives.

Humanity is all connected. One life is connected with so many other lives. None of us is an island; therefore, your vision will compel you to take someone along on the journey.

Perhaps you will impact customers in a way that has never been attempted before. You may create a product that the world is longing for, write a book that moves the reader to make real change, start a business that meets a need in your city, state, country, or around the world, or start a non-profit that relieves suffering. Whatever your vision, whatever your passion, it won't lift off without your ability to take others along.

Who are the people who should be on the journey? Whom do you influence? What group of people is desperate for your message?

In my banking business, the vision is to create the most incredible banking experience for the clients while creating a world-class work environment for the employees. Executing on this vision demands a clear understanding of our clients: What do they expect? How do they expect to be treated? What products and services will they demand? How will they want those products and services delivered? It also requires a very clear idea of the employee's expectations: What tools are being provided? What work environment is being established? How do the employees expect to be treated? What motivates them to go above and beyond? Finally, management needs to be assessed: What support can be provided? Are the decisions close enough to the customer to allow for immediate impact? Does management's vision line up with or provide autonomy for fulfilling the vision?

At every level, executing the vision will require that people be considered and brought along. Taking each of these groups on a journey and impacting their lives along the way will ensure the vision is fulfilled. Your vision or any vision that is destiny-bound will involve taking others along.

INFLUENCING OTHERS

Because leadership is about the influence you gain over others to help them get where they are going or get you where you are going, your vision will have an influence component. It will require you to learn the art of influence and the heavy responsibility that comes along with holding that position.

As you begin to unveil your innermost desires and dreams in the form of a vision for your life, people will be attracted like metal to a magnet. True vision is inspiring, self-sacrificing, and a powerful motivator. Vision begins to take on a life and mission in a way that communicates a mandate for movement to those who hear. Create a movement and people will be attracted to it.

Think about someone you know who has a vision—someone who could see what others couldn't; someone who would do what others wouldn't. Whether this person was a humanitarian on television communicating a cause, someone in your community talking about changes that would enhance lives in the local area, or a business leader whose product or service would revolutionize the world, that visionary was infectious. Being around someone with a vision is an amazing catalyst for you to join in moving humanity toward greatness.

Vision put a man on the moon. Vision took man into flight. Vision brought us the first horseless carriage. Vision built the banking system. Vision has cared for the orphans in India. Vision will catapult your life from where you are right now to where you want to be, and that vision will influence the lives of so many others.

The world is waiting for your vision. It can't wait to see what will be birthed in your life. We wait anxiously for you to unveil the greatness in you because when you do, it will influence the people all around you.

Let me remind you that just a few years ago, we were all carrying bulky cell phones. Even in their more compact flip style, they were bulky and performed only a couple of functions. They had a contact list, could dial a phone number, take a few pictures, text a message, and maybe a few other functions. In addition, we were carrying daytimers or PDAs. To get simple directions, we had to print them off the Internet before leaving a location or take a map with us on the trip. Then Steve Jobs had a vision—a vision that transformed an industry; a vision that brought all these devices together to eliminate the need to carry multiple ones. The iPhone is a fully integrated music player, cell phone, calendar, map, and device with countless other functions. Jobs' vision forever changed the handheld device business and influenced an entire generation. We now have i-everything. People of every age use the bestselling iPhone as their device. Jobs' vision didn't just improve on the cell phone; it influenced nearly every aspect of the personal computer, business strategy, marketing, distribution, and wireless industries and the people in them.

Jobs' vision had influence. Maybe your vision won't be as globally recognized as the iPhone; nonetheless, it will have influence over people and transform their lives. Your vision, your dream, will affect people everywhere. It will be world-changing.

CHANGING THE WORLD

How far will your vision reach? How do you know it's going in the right direction? Often, developing a vision will have a global component and be big enough to break the barriers of country borders. Another vision blocker really comes in the form of seeing your vision as too small. Acts 1:8 says, "you will be made witnesses to Jerusalem, Judea and to the ends of the earth." Jerusalem represents your local community, Judea represents your state or country, and the ends of the earth represents a global impact.

You have been designed to make a global impact. Your vision will have a global component. Don't be tempted to run with a vision that only includes you or a small group of people in your local area. There is a whole world that needs what you bring to the table.

You have done so much work to remove the obstacles to your destiny, ridding your life of vision blockers not so you can make local impact, but so you can make global impact. You are created with greatness and world-changing power.

Consider the "American Girl" story. Pleasant Rowland, a creative history teacher, wanted to find a way to teach young girls American history in a fun way that made lasting impact. She spent time as a textbook writer, attempting to create textbooks that would tell the story in a more exciting and colorful way. Then she formed the Pleasant Company and began manufacturing her American Girl dolls, each one accompanied by a book that told a story from the girl doll's point of view. She began to market her dolls in the local area, selling them to students and their parents. Today, what she envisioned as a way to teach American history to young girls has grown into a global business. Recently, American Girl stores have opened in Canada and other countries are slated to come onboard. In 2012, American Girl reported sales of over $246 million and growing.

Pleasant Rowland had an admirable vision, one worth pursuing that has resulted in forever changing the way history is taught. Her vision began locally but expanded to being global. When you see your vision from a global perspective, it brings a completely different dimension to your life and takes the limits off of your pursuits.

To make a global impact, your vision should pass a few tests:

1. **Does the vision lead a revolution or reformation?** When you look forward to living out this vision, does it make a change that will impact or reform people?

2. **Does the vision result in a positive change in people's lives?** Will humanity be better because you are doing what you do? Will your vision help them reach higher, dream bigger, live more passionately, or free them from some atrocity?

3. **Do you have the passion to push through any barrier?** Does your vision spark enough passion in you to cause you to do what no one else is willing to do, and to keep doing it despite any opposition that might arise?

4. **Is it motivated in Love?** The most compelling force on the planet is Love. Love has the ability to change every circumstance, soften the hardest critic, create the most passionate followers, and build the strongest commitment. My wife always says, "People will let you help them only after they know you love them." So, is your dream motivated by Love?

Passing through this test puts your vision on a global scale and gets you ready to change the world. You have been designed to go to the ends of the earth and live the life you've been dreaming about.

SUMMARY

Leadership is powerful. The ability to move people in a positive direction and accomplish world-changing results is amazing. Leading with vision is exponentially incredible and has the ability to conquer so many different things. Your vision now unblocked, free, and released in your life has the ability to accomplish the impossible and forever change the life you have been leading and the lives of those around you. Once you find your direction and gain a clear understanding of the path you are taking, it should compel you to take others with you, influence the world around you, and change that world forever.

Henry and Richard Blackaby, in their book *Spiritual Leadership*, define leadership as "Seeing where others are supposed to be and helping them get there." My challenge to you is to find that direction, take others along, and go make a global impact!

CHAPTER 13

Finding Your Purpose

"If you can't figure out your purpose, figure out your passion.
For your passion will lead you right into your purpose."

— Bishop T.D. Jakes

The last three chapters have been about taking the next steps once you identify your vision blockers, so you can release your destiny. You have learned how to make lasting change, find your moral authority, and lead with vision. Overcoming your vision blockers has released a new sense of power and authority in your life. You truly do count, and what you do with your life does make a difference. I hope excitement and anticipation are building in you as you begin to believe more and more that you can conquer and become unstoppable in your life.

In this chapter, you will discover the foundation for finding your purpose. Throughout this world, countless millions of people are saying, "I was going to...," "I could have been...," "I should be...," or "I am so bored, confused, frustrated, and tired of being what I am." A life without purpose is an accidental exercise in frustration with a lack of fulfillment.

Consider the story of Frank, a military officer. Frank graduated with honors from the military academy and was recognized as "most likely to succeed." He spent years in the military and rapidly rose up the chain of command. He took command of several large units and led them with passion and principle. When he was recognized with a distinguished service medal, he was part of a beautiful and well-choreographed ceremony. His family and friends attended the ceremony to show support for his efforts. After the ceremony, however, Frank told his family, friends, and close supporters, "I am sorry! I really don't know the person who just received that award. I am not sure why, but none of this makes any sense to me any longer. I am leading on principle but not with passion. There is something in me that says I've missed something in my life." Frank went on to say, "I don't know who I am or where I'm going. I want to be alive and live with exuberance." Frank felt empty, hollow, and like just a shell of himself. The guy who had been celebrated in high school, college, and the military had become empty and confused.

There are so many people like Frank. We have all probably met a Frank; in fact, we might be Frank. Everything is going well—you are at the top of your field and being recognized for the contributions you have made—and yet you have no idea why.

Or consider this story of a young woman named Rachel. Because she was the product of an unplanned pregnancy, Rachel lived her life knowing she was the "accident" and her mother treated her as such. She developed scars and wounds from constantly being reminded that she was not a planned event. Had her mother not gone to that party and drank so much, Rachel wouldn't have been alive. Rachel was raised by a single mother who had to work two jobs just to make ends meet, and the only place her mother could afford to live was in the dangerous part of town. Because Rachel's mother was frustrated with her mistakes and the decisions she had made that put her in this position, she took it out on Rachel, daily blaming her daughter for being the reason for her problems. Something inside of Rachel screamed for something different. Unconfident, confused, and angry, Rachel had no idea why she was born into the situation she was in. She had no idea which way to go, and every path seemed to lead to hopelessness. Nothing seemed right and nothing seemed to be giving a stamp of approval to move forward. "Why am I here?" Rachel would scream.

Millions are impacted by circumstances similar to Rachel's. Certainly, a mistake has been made. This situation definitely can't be right. Rachel is not alone. "Why am I here?" is a question that plagues countless people around the world. Something inside me tells me that there must be a reason. There must be a purpose for my and everyone's existence. What on earth could that purpose be?

EVERYONE IS HERE FOR A PURPOSE

Before Thomas Alva Edison invented the incandescent lightbulb, he failed a thousand times in his attempts to find the right materials and design to invent it. Throughout all these failures, his mind stayed focused on the purpose: to fill a room with light in a sustainable and cost-effective way that did not require burning candles or having a fire. Edison knew his purpose long before he created the lightbulb. He just needed to find the right material to fulfill it.

In Psalms 139:13-18, the inventor's knowledge of his creation is described eloquently:

> For You formed my inward parts;
> You covered me in my mother's womb.
> I will praise You, for I am fearfully *and* wonderfully made;

Marvelous are Your works,
And *that* my soul knows very well.
My frame was not hidden from You,
When I was made in secret,
And skillfully wrought in the lowest parts of the earth.
Your eyes saw my substance, being yet unformed.
And in Your book they all were written,
The days fashioned for me,
When *as yet there were* none of them.
How precious also are Your thoughts to me, O God!
How great is the sum of them!
If I should count them, they would be more in number than
the sand;
When I awake, I am still with You.

The designer has a purpose for you; regardless of where you have been or where you come from, you have been placed on this planet for a reason. Just like a car is to be driven, planes are to fly, and space shuttles are to explore space, your life is designed to fulfill a purpose. If a car doesn't move, a plane doesn't fly, or a space shuttle is never launched, each of these creations' existence has no meaning. It's when the creation is used for its designed purpose that everything makes sense, life is enhanced, and fulfillment is gained.

Discovering your purpose brings to your life the meaning you desperately seek. Author Myles Munroe said, "Without purpose, life is an experiment or a haphazard journey that results in frustration, disappointment, and failure." Finding and fulfilling your purpose must be the primary and relentlessly pursued goal of every person. Meaning and fulfillment lie in discovering your purpose.

What are you here to accomplish? Why have you been designed and placed right where you are? What reason do you have for living? When you die, for what will you be remembered? When these questions begin to have answers and you begin living passionately to answer them you begin to change your story into one of success and fulfillment.

Make no mistake; you are here to fulfill a purpose.

What is "purpose"? The word is defined as: "the reason for which something exists or is done, made, used, etc.; an intended or desired result, end, aim, or goal; the point of the issue; the object, point, or rationale; the aim or goal of a person; something that has to be attained or done."

All of these definitions lead us to the same conclusion. If you are alive and breathing, you exist, and if you exist, you have a purpose. No mistake, no error, no accident!

No matter whether you are the product of an accidental pregnancy like me, were raised in the midst of hopeless poverty, come from an affluent family, were adopted, were orphaned, or were raised by a loving, caring family, the same is true: you are here; therefore, you have a purpose, and it's time to find it.

ASKING YOURSELF THE RIGHT QUESTIONS

Are you satisfied with what you have created in your life or where your life has brought you? Have you been successful in the eyes of those around you, but something isn't quite right? What could possibly be the problem? Consider the motivation behind what you have been doing for so many years. Is there substance to what you have been building, or are you building for the mere reason that you can and so you do?

Are you pursuing something without a purpose? For example, perhaps you are pursuing wealth. There is no doubt that wealth can help perpetuate a vision or mission. Financial independence is a worthwhile goal well within your grasp that you are more than capable of achieving. There is nothing wrong with a drive that reaches for this goal. What leaves an emptiness in your heart is striving for financial gain when that alone is your reason for living.

Following are the right questions you should be asking yourself to determine your true reason for living.

Question 1: Are you seeking success or fulfillment?

Fulfilling your purpose in life and becoming crystal clear about what that purpose looks like will provide lifelong fulfillment and a sense of meaning that goes beyond worldly success. Worldly success has become the focus of everything corporate, everything educational, and everything in the media. As a result, success has gained a skewed definition. Success today means attaining monetary gain, building a global business, and becoming an iconic leader with global recognition. While these things are not bad, what about the individual who founds an orphanage with a desire to place young kids in great homes with parents who can't have children of their own? What about missionaries who bring medical supplies, food, and aid to suffering Third World countries? Consider the work of Pastor Ruben Reyna of Living Word Christian Center. His life's work, aside from building a life-changing congregation in Los Angeles, has been building a great recovery program. Pastor Ruben has founded several men and women's homes in southern California that take gang members, convicted felons, alcoholics, drug abusers, and really anyone whom society would consider a "throwaway" or indigent. He has built a program that helps each of these individuals detox, recover, gain employment, learn skills, and find purpose in life. His program is so successful that the judicial system is now assigning convicted people to it for recovery and sentencing. Pastor Ruben has an 85 percent recovery and rehabilitation rate, which exceeds the standard penal system's rate multiple times over. He has no fame, no fortune, no world notoriety, and yet, Pastor Ruben is one of the most successful people I have known.

What are you searching for?

Question 2: Are you seeking prestige or purpose?

How do others see you? What position have you gained that others recognize as powerful and prominent? More importantly, "How important is that prestige to you?" Prestige is often a motivation for others to perform and conquer the tasks and challenges that present themselves. To be seen in others' eyes as someone with standing and position can be a shallow motivation for accomplishing great feats. Prestige is, by definition: achieving standing or estimation in others' eyes; to have weight or credibility in general opinion; or to command a position in people's minds. Prestige can be gained by any admirable accomplishment or be due to popular opinion, regardless of the accomplishment associated with its attribution.

Finding yourself in a position of prestige is not a bad place to be or a goal unworthy of pursuit. But prestige alone will not satisfy you. Inherent in prestige's foundation is that it is all about what other people think of you and the things you have done. When people are for you, it is fantastic, wonderful, and produces a sense of great accomplishment. But what about the moments when people are not for you? What happens when eyes are not looking in your direction? Does that in some way devalue your life's work, your passion, or your life's mission? I think not! Seeking others' admiration or being concerned about their admonition is a poor foundation from which to build a strong sense of purpose. While your vision will influence and impact other people, searching for their approval will not satisfy your soul's deep desire.

"You have been fearfully and wonderfully made." That statement stands on its own. Regardless of other people's opinions or approval, you have been created wonderfully to accomplish so many things and change the world.

The problem with prestige that is formed from others' opinions is that those opinions are based upon partial information. Others can't possibly know the passion burning in your heart. They are not fully educated on your position or what you believe your cause is going to be. They can't know the feeling of unresolved emotion that goes along with not pursuing your purpose. Those with opinions are speaking about you with only partial evidence, so they can't come to a conclusive position regarding what you want to do. This basis alone is enough to realize that pursuing purpose is more powerful than prestige.

Let prestige emerge out of following your purpose. Allow prestige to follow the work you do to change the world and conquer your dreams. Don't pursue prestige; pursue purpose.

Question 3: What is my real motivation? What is my heart crying out to do?

After Frank, the military officer whose story I told earlier, confessed that he didn't know who he was, he went on to say that since he was a little boy, he had dreamed of writing music and playing his guitar. He was a psalmist who wanted to write music that would inspire a generation and ease the suffering of those in pain. During the many years he had been pursuing his military career and receiving accolades and prestige, his heart had been crying out to write and play music—music that would cause its listeners to take action in their lives. All that time, he had been denying his true purpose.

What moves you? What takes your breath away? What do you want so desperately that it makes a physiological difference in your life—you can't sleep when you think about it; you can't take a deep breath; you have butterflies in your stomach; you can't eat, and not doing it drives you to tears? By pursuing the answers to those questions, you can find your purpose.

Take some time and answer these questions for yourself.

Do I want success or fulfillment? What means the most to me?

Can I gain success out of fulfillment? How would that take place?

The last time I won an award, was I more concerned with the accomplishment or the praise from others? Describe how you felt.

How important are other people's opinions to me?

What really motivates me?

_____

_____

If I were to write down all the things I would like to do, which would bring me to tears?

_____

_____

IDENTIFYING YOUR PASSION

Pastor Andy Stanley said, "Vision goes beyond what could be done. It is something that should be done. It is something that *must* happen." Vision is about gaining a clear idea of your purpose, which is motivated by your passion. As Bishop T.D. Jakes said, "If you can't find your purpose, find your passion; it will lead you to your purpose." Passion and purpose work together, so if we can begin to identify what moves you, what it is you will do anything to accomplish, we will have found your passion; from there we can find your purpose, and then your vision will emerge.

An Old Testament story illustrates this concept well. The speaker here, Nehemiah, is the cupbearer to the King of the Persians, and one of the many Jews who had been led into captivity in Babylon. The passage opens when he hears bad news from his homeland.

> It came to pass in the month of Chislev, in the twentieth year, as I was in Shushan the citadel, that Hanani one of my brethren came with men from Judah; and I asked them concerning the Jews who had escaped, who had survived the captivity, and concerning Jerusalem. And they said to me, "The survivors who are left from the captivity in the province are there in great distress and reproach. The wall of Jerusalem is also broken down,

and its gates are burned with fire." So it was, when I heard these words, that I sat down and wept, and mourned for many days; I was fasting and praying before the God of heaven. And I said: "I pray, Lord God of heaven, O great and awesome God, You who keep Your covenant and mercy with those who love You and observe Your commandments, please let Your ear be attentive and Your eyes open, that You may hear the prayer of Your servant which I pray before You now, day and night, for the children of Israel Your servants, and confess the sins of the children of Israel which we have sinned against You. Both my father's house and I have sinned. We have acted very corruptly against You, and have not kept the commandments, the statutes, nor the ordinances which You commanded Your servant Moses. Remember, I pray, the word that You commanded Your servant Moses, saying, 'If you are unfaithful, I will scatter you among the nations; but if you return to Me, and keep My commandments and do them, though some of you were cast out to the farthest part of the heavens, yet I will gather them from there, and bring them to the place which I have chosen as a dwelling for My name.' Now these are Your servants and Your people, whom You have redeemed by Your great power, and by Your strong hand. O Lord, I pray, please let Your ear be attentive to the prayer of Your servant, and to the prayer of Your servants who desire to fear Your name; and let Your servant prosper this day, I pray, and grant him mercy in the sight of this man." (Nehemiah 1)

Nehemiah was so upset by the tragedy being experienced by his people that he couldn't eat or sleep. Instead, he cried out to the Lord, praying for and building a strategy to help his people. Nehemiah also did not possess the freedom most of us do. He was living as a prisoner in a foreign land, serving a king who did not hold the same beliefs as he and his people did. He was at the mercy of this king.

Living a life without purpose and not connecting with our purpose can feel just as incarcerating as Nehemiah must have felt. We may also be servant to a king (job, boss, lifestyle) that doesn't share our passion or convictions.

Your passion will move you. It will be all that you can think about and all that you can dream about. I am sure you can identify what drives you to move. The terror in his homeland drove Nehemiah to take action by asking the king for permission to rebuild Jerusalem, and when it was granted, returning home to do the work despite all the obstacles that stood in his way.

It is amazing what passion can do. It's a force that helps people move from mediocre to extraordinary. Passion is a fuel that burns hotter than jet fuel and is extremely combustible. It will ignite into a vision that produces action to make change. Finding your passion will lead you to your purpose and produce for you a vision that makes you unstoppable.

What are you moved to tears about? What would make you fast, pray, meditate, dream, and take action like Nehemiah did?

_____

_____

_____

TAKING ACTION!

How many times have you had a great idea only to hear someone else bring that idea to market? You come up with a great product or service, something the world can't live without, but you do nothing to make it become reality. Then several months go by, and on the radio, you hear a commercial for that very product or service. What's the difference between you and the person selling the product? Action!

Nothing happens without action. You took great action by purchasing and reading this book. You can get thoroughly inspired to overcome your vision blockers and pursue your passion, but if you do nothing, nothing will change. Nehemiah was moved to take action. He devised a solution and went before the king to present his desire. The king not only granted the desire but bankrolled the project. As Bruce Lee once said, "If you spend too much time thinking about a thing, you'll never get it done." You can think about it, analyze it, strategize about it, devise solutions for it, come up with contingency plans, but if you never execute on it, all of it is in vain and will never be accomplished.

Get motivated! The time to act on your dream is right now. The time to create great wealth is right now. The time to pursue that vision is right now. What are you waiting for? What is getting in your way?

Anything you come up with is an excuse. Nothing should stand in your way! James 1:22 says, "Do not merely listen to the word, and so deceive yourself. Do what it says." You can apply that so directly to your life. You have identified what you want out of life. You spent time getting a clear and concise understanding of your purpose. Your vision has become clear enough to see where you want to go. Stopping here would be deceiving yourself. You could convince yourself falsely that you have arrived. But truth dictates that the action is where you are judged. The old quote says, "You will be judged by your actions, not your intentions."

It is true that intentions never changed anyone's life. Intent never brought wealth to anyone. Intent never built a house or founded a company. Intent is a fairy tale waiting for action to accompany it. Only by action does accomplishment take place.

You can do it! Do it today!

BELIEVE IT!

Another vision blocker chapter titled "Overcoming Self-Doubt" could have been added to this book considering the number of people who allow their own doubts to stop their progress. At this point in your journey, you already realize you are here for something; you have been given passion to accomplish greatness and your vision is revealed. You are at the point where you must be a believer in your own destiny. How do you make yourself into your first believer? What are the steps to feeling confident that you can and will accomplish what you set out to do?

I am going to give you six goals that will help you overcome self-doubt and start believing in yourself:

1. **Stop making excuses:** Every reason you can devise for not moving forward is just an excuse keeping you from realizing your dream. Stop making excuses now. Instead, make the commitment that there will be no more excuses. Decide that not one reason exists to keep you from moving forward.

2. **Stop listening to others:** Well-intentioned people will tell you that your ideas are silly. There will be criticism and contention for the journey you are about to take. Stop listening to them. Silence them in your life. Listen to your heart and hear what it has to say.

3. **Know your inner circle:** Find your mentor, coach, and cheerleaders and only allow them to help guide you as you go forward.

4. **Stop needing validation:** You don't need *anyone's* approval to execute on your vision. The only approval you need is your own. The need for validation is born out of insecurity and a lack of confidence. As of today, you now believe in your ability to accomplish the vision you have been given.

5. **Don't talk too much about your plans:** In the next chapter, I am going to talk about going public with your vision. Communicating your vision is powerful, but don't talk too much about the details and inner workings of your vision or you will only give fuel to the flame of opinion. You don't need to share too much. Cast your vision without revealing the strategic plan to everyone.

6. **Just Start Going!:** Belief is born out of experience. The more you do something, the better you become at doing it. I mentioned in Chapter 5: Overcoming Fear that the best way to overcome your fear is to do what you are afraid to do, a lot. Just start! Start right now. Do something today that begins to move you in the direction of your dream. Why wait? Just start going!

You are awesome! You are unstoppable! You are a force to reckon with, and the world has no idea what is about to hit it. Believe in yourself and stop doubting.

I was counseling a business owner who was just about to buy his first business. He had done months of research, scrutinized the financials, interviewed the staff, talked with clients, and was confident it was a business he wanted to own. Right before closing the transaction, doubt began to settle in. Questions arose like: "How am I ever going to run this business? What do I know about this industry? What was I thinking?" After talking to him for some time, I helped him to understand that he would win. I knew he could because, just like when he was in college and winning every race and conquering in his sport because he had put in the time to train, worked on strategy, developed a plan, taken care of his health, and identified his competition, he had done the same in preparing to acquire this business. He studied, trained, and developed a plan for this business, so in short order, he was going to win there as well.

You can do it!

SUMMARY

Your life has been waiting for this moment. Every vision blocker has been overcome. You have dealt with each one so effectively and found a place of strength by making lasting change and finding your moral authority. You know from whence you came, and you know that you have definitely been put here on purpose for a purpose.

There is no such thing as an accident as it relates to humanity. Because you are here proves that you have a purpose and you have been designed with greatness. Like the automobile designed for the purpose of moving people around and the plane designed to fly, you have been designed to pursue your purpose with passion, leading to a vision that changes the world. Believe it! Act on it!

Just Do It!

CHAPTER 14

Embracing Your Vision

"Write the vision
And make it plain on tablets,
That he may run who reads it.
For the vision is yet for an appointed time;
But at the end it will speak,
and it will not lie.
Though it tarries, wait for it;
Because it will surely come,
It will not tarry."

— Habakkuk 2:2-3

Now that you have come to the end of this book, you may be asking yourself, "What are the next steps for this newly emerging visionary?" Hopefully, at this point you realize that you possess the power to overcome your vision blockers; you have truly removed any barriers to your success, implemented permanent change strategies, and enlisted the support of strategic partners who will guide your success as you move beyond this point. In the last couple of chapters, you have worked through leading with your vision and finding your purpose to bring clarity to your mission. In this final chapter, you will learn how to embrace fully your vision and make it a part of your everyday life.

WRITE IT DOWN, MAKING IT PLAIN

Do you know what you want to accomplish in this life? By now, you should be gaining a better understanding of what you are here to do. The next step is to write it down. Putting pen to paper and actually writing down your vision begins to bring it to life.

In this chapter's opening quote, God tells Habakkuk to "write the vision and make it plain." Habakkuk is to write down what is to be accomplished and put it in plain language so all can understand. Similarly, you need to write down your vision in language you can understand.

Your written vision will take on some very serious characteristics as you put pen to paper and record what you expect to be accomplished. These characteristics are:

1. **The Vision Becomes Official:** a vision that is simply spoken and never written down is unofficial and serves as a pipe dream. There is no commitment to a verbal vision, it takes on no ownership, and it is easily forgotten, changed, or maneuvered around. But once you commit that vision to paper, it becomes official. The law for your life. That written word takes on life as a mandate that must be executed and delivered upon. In ancient times when kings made laws or cast judgments, one job was vitally important to the process: the scribe was responsible for recording all that the king spoke. Decisions, strategies, and directives were written so they could be communicated to the constituents in the kingdom. What was spoken and transcribed became laws that all were responsible for upholding. Your written vision takes on the same life. You put it down and

it becomes something that all of your being begins to uphold and bring to pass.

2. **The Vision Becomes Visual:** Writing the vision down keeps it in front of you at all times. There is an old English saying, based on the Scripture in Matthew: "The eyes are the window to the soul." What you gaze upon begins to write itself on your heart. When you see the vision in front of you every day, when you remind your soul of what you believe is the mission for your life, it begins to translate into action that becomes reality. You may have heard of people who want a certain car or home, so they keep a picture on the refrigerator or on the front door so they can look at it often during the day. Seeing that picture reminds your heart to do things that will cause you to attain that goal. Your vision operates much the same way. Writing it down causes you to focus your heart, soul, mind, and attention in that direction. You begin to make decisions for your life based on achieving that vision.

3. **The Vision Becomes Permanent:** Writing the vision down creates a sense of permanency. By recording your vision on paper, it no longer has the property of change. While you can erase and start over the process, writing it down makes you much more conscious of it than you would be of a verbal vision that can change every time you speak it to someone. Verbal visions become an unrealized dream while a written vision becomes something permanent to execute. I can remember doing consulting for a startup company a few years ago. The owners were doubting the value of using a written business plan with financial projections. In the business world, a written business plan is in essence a written vision. You are projecting what you want your company to look like as you grow that company. The owners didn't understand the power of writing it down, and they debated with me the validity of this process. After

much discussion, I finally persuaded them to write the plan before starting the business. They did a great job working on the various sections, including the financial projections. As the company began its operations and took on new and vibrant life, I would consult with the owners to ensure they were moving ahead appropriately and taking the necessary actions. Much to their surprise, they were making financial decisions based on the projections written in their plan. As we discussed the addition of new equipment, I asked, "Why are you purchasing this equipment now?" My response shocked them both. They replied, "Because in our projections, we predicted a certain level of revenue before adding new equipment; the new equipment will be necessary to stage our growth; we have hit that consistently, and based on our projections and business plan, it's time to add equipment." The company has grown phenomenally and sold to a larger firm for a profit. But if the owners had not written down their vision, they wouldn't have had a basis for executing it. Your written vision becomes a permanent document that you will execute against.

4. **The Vision Transfers Action from Head to Heart and from Heart to Head:** When you take the time to write the vision, you're taking the step of combining your heart and head in one unified commitment. To write the vision engages the head on the appropriate structure that should be communicated. It also engages the heart to determine what should be written. This transfer between head and heart creates a bond that requires action. Your head will continue thinking about what was written, and your heart moves your emotions to take action against those thoughts. You are building an internal military that creates a strategy for proper execution. Proverbs 3:3 says, "Let not mercy and truth forsake you, bind them around your neck, write them on the tablet of your heart." An amazing inexpli-

cable transfer takes place when you write down your vision. You begin to transcribe it right on your heart, and the heart creates an action plan.

Hopefully, you have been convinced that to embrace your vision, you must write it down. The first step is getting it on paper in front of you. Write a rough first draft that may or may not be coherent. Just get it down. Whatever your heart tells you, your head can find the words to express to bring reason and explanation to it, so write it down. And finally, make it plain. You don't have to use the most eloquent wording or most exhaustive intellectual words ever written. Just make it plain so those who read it can run with it—so they can understand and get excited about what you are about to accomplish.

It doesn't have to be complex to be great. Writing it in plain language that is easily understood won't complicate it for you, and it will allow others to get behind it. Earlier, you learned that people are waiting to follow the vision you have, but you have to communicate it plainly for each one to understand. Use words that can be understood by all who may read it. The vision doesn't have to be wordy either—a few words, if they communicate your life's vision, can be powerful. A vision like "I will eradicate hunger in the Pacific Northwest" can be a powerful vision for all to understand. Maybe yours is "I will start a new business that will provide _____ services to elementary school children across America." Whatever the vision, just write it down plainly.

Take a shot at writing it down now. On the lines below, write down what you believe to be your vision. By the way, I'm excited for you; you've overcome the vision blockers so you can take this magnificent step of writing your vision:

_____

_____

_____

_____

_____

_____

COMMUNICATE IT EVERYWHERE

As you learned in Chapter 12: Leading with Vision, the objective is to take people with you on the journey. Helping them get from where they are to where they are supposed to be or even going along on your journey will demand that you communicate your vision everywhere. As John Maxwell says in his book *The 21 Irrefutable Laws of Leadership*, "Anyone can steer the ship, but it takes a leader to chart the course." Maxwell goes on to discuss the leader's role in communicating that course effectively. In order to get your vision to fruition, you have to communicate: loudly, plainly, everywhere, and often.

When you begin to communicate, you will inspire others to go along on the journey. You will inspire others with the conviction you have to get there. You will enlist support to finance, perpetuate, and assist in fulfilling the vision. People follow a movement, and more importantly, follow a mission.

Communicating your vision effectively requires four components:

1. **Plainly Spoken:** The vision should be clear enough that all who hear it can understand what you want to accomplish. It should be communicated plainly enough to garner support.

2. **Precise:** One of the tragedies of vision communication is that the vision is so complex and scattered that those who hear it can't comprehend it. If it is too elaborate, trying to wrap your mind around it and find your connection with others will fail. Speak the vision very precisely and simply so your listeners can understand what you want to accomplish.

3. **Provide Opportunity:** So often, great vision is not supported because the listener can't understand how to connect or get involved. Your goal is to enlist support—emotional, financial, or physical—to move your vision forward. If the listener doesn't know how to connect with you, he or she won't. People take the path of least resistance, so if it's too complicated to get involved in your mission, they will wait until the next one comes along.

4. **Purpose Focused:** Your communication should focus on the why behind the vision. Tell the story that led you to have this vision. Remember the words of Andy Stanley, "A vision is born out of a desire that something must be done about a condition in life." If something must be done, communicating why it's unacceptable and why this vision will address the issues is a requirement for enlisting support to bring about its successful completion.

Your vision is so powerful that you must communicate it everywhere. To reach the goals, dreams, and life that you want, this vision should be included in everything you talk about or write about. It should encompass every part of your life.

Communicate at parties, to your family, on the Internet, by email, through video, whatever it takes to get this message out everywhere possible. It's time to let the world know what you intend to do. Communicate everywhere and often.

You have already taken the step to write down your vision; the next mandate of success is to communicate it often. How often? The litmus test is that as soon as you think you are getting sick of hearing yourself say it, others are just beginning to understand and get on board. Casting and re-casting your vision to your family, your church, your organization, or your employees keeps the message in front of everyone and gives people the objectives that need to be reached. You continue to explain what you see so they can see it too. You communicate what you expect until they expect it too. You communicate what you want until they want it too.

Communicate subtly and dramatically as often as humanly possible. Don't stop. Soon you will notice the realization of your vision. Not only will you see it, but everyone around you will become an owner as each one sees it for his or her life as well. Now you are creating a tribe of people headed in the same direction with the same underlying mission that will be achieved.

List some ways that you can communicate your vision.

_____   _____
_____   _____
_____   _____
_____   _____

ENLIST YOUR RUNNERS

Habakkuk 2:2 says to write down the vision plainly "that he may run who reads it." Runners are those who have read the vision and are so compelled to see it completed that they will join the fight to make it a reality. This verse describes those who read the vision being so moved regarding the mission that a sense of urgency has taken over and they begin, not to walk, but run toward its execution.

Who are the runners for your vision? When you begin to communicate the vision, there will be those who read it, hear it, and understand it who will be moved with an urgency to help complete it. A serious mistake made by visionaries is not to identify the runners. Runners are a very specific and necessary part of realizing any dream.

Think about the development of the mega social network Facebook. Mark Zuckerberg had a vision to connect people around the world in one space that reveals who they are and what they like. He was the impetus, the technical genius, behind Facebook's launch. But had it not been for Eduardo Saverin, who provided the initial capital; Sean Parker, who operated as its first president and connected Mark to venture capital; and the many other early dorm roommates of Mark, Facebook may not be the social force we all know it to be today. Eduardo, Sean, and the other early founders served as Facebook's runners.

People who hear the vision, see the vision, get excited about the vision, and can make connections, enlist others' support, and continue to communicate the vision with urgency are necessary for any vision's fulfillment. Runners run with you. They are the people who believe in the vision and can exponentially move the vision from paper to reality.

Who are your runners? Who are the people who will run with your vision and help move you to levels you haven't dreamed about before?

A significant part of embracing your vision is finding and recruiting your runners who will continue to assist in materializing your vision. Without runners, the message continues to be the project you work on alone. I would like to remind you that you are here to impact humanity and the world is waiting for you. The products you develop, the money you raise, the lives you touch through coaching, mentoring, or counseling are all waiting for you to move this project beyond yourself and take it to the world. Runners allow you to do that and do it more efficiently, more urgently, and in a timelier manner.

Embrace your vision and find your runners!

KEEPING IT BURNING

I believe one of the most overwhelming reasons for failure is that people quit entirely too soon. Right before the big break, the discouragement may feel overwhelming, there is no instant gratification, the financing seems to be running out, and doubt can set in—"Maybe I didn't have the right idea to begin with, and therefore, I can stop." Whatever the excuse, let me say simply, "Do Not Quit!"

I am reminded of a story Napoleon Hill relates in his book *Think and Grow Rich*. A gold prospector had purchased tools and begun the job of digging for gold during the California Gold Rush. Day after day, month after month, he dug for gold, only to come up with nothing but dirt and rocks. Fully discouraged and irritated by his failed effort, he sold all his tools to a junk man for only a few hundred dollars. After the disappointed prospector went home in disgust, the astute junk man hired a mining engineer who checked the mine and calculated that there was a vein of gold just three feet from where the previous prospector stopped digging. The junk man went on to make millions, extracting the ore from the mine while the previous prospector went home with nothing but the few hundred dollars.

Earlier I mentioned how Thomas Edison made one thousand attempts before he succeeded in creating the lightbulb. Had Edison given up at 999, he never would have discovered the one that worked. Had the prospector kept digging, he would have dramatically changed his life forever. The point of these stories is: You must keep the fire burning and never give up. I love the quote by Henry Ford that says, "Whether you think you can or think you can't, you are right."

The time for you vision is now. Don't let anything get in your way or stop you from achieving your best life. You can do it. Reinforce yourself by reading what you wrote, reviewing what you are communicating, recasting your vision, running with your runners, and fanning the flame. I challenge you to keep your vision in front of you and to keep feeding it with confidence. You can make it happen!

You are the one who can and will make your dream a reality. I believe in you and pray that you believe in yourself. I can't wait to see how you change the world and reach for your destiny by making your dream a reality.

God Bless!

A FINAL NOTE

Moving Mountains

"Faith moves mountains but you have to keep pushing
while you are praying."

— Mason Cooley

Hopefully, as a result of reading this book, you have gained some revelations about where your life has been, and more importantly, where your life is going. You should not be overwhelmed by the possibilities that lie ahead, but have gained confidence that you are called to achieving them. Each of us exists to accomplish something very specific related to humanity. That something will lead you to prosperity, love, admiration, and fulfillment beyond your imagination. It is so powerful when a vision exists in the mind and heart of someone who will take action to achieve it. So the question becomes: What will you do?

As a result of reading the last fourteen chapters and realizing that you too can overcome your vision blockers, what will you do to make a difference in your own life? Your vision requires you to take action in order to achieve it. Your heart has already been telling you that something needs to change; your mind has already seen the possibilities of living differently, making more money, and touching humanity in powerful and profound ways. So the question is: What will you do? Does this just become another book that got you inspired but never got you motivated, or is this the point in your life where excuses end and action begins? Those are powerful questions. I realize they are a bit "in your face," but I have never been the kind of person who doesn't deal in truth. John 8:32 says, "The truth will set you free," and I believe that to be the case. Hearing that someone else will fulfill your vision or that it's okay to stay the same is not good enough for me. I believe in so much more for you. I believe that in you is the next great invention, the next iPod/iPhone, the next economic breakthrough, the next design for transportation that will touch humanity in a great way. I believe you hold the key to ending world hunger, taking back the streets from gang violence, volunteering to help the youth in your community. I believe you are the one, but the question is: What do you believe and will you take action to prove it?

You have read through chapters giving you strategies to overcome vision blockers, encouraging you to take action, and inspiring you to embrace your vision. Take a minute now and write down your Top Ten list—the top ten things you will do as a result of reading this book:

1. _____

2. _____

3. _____

4. _____

5. _____

6. _____

7. _____

8. _____

9. _____

10. _____

Next, I want to encourage you to do something bold. I would like you to contact me and let me know what you liked about what you read. I would even like to know what you didn't like. I want to improve myself and be able to help more people. Most of all, I want to know the stories of your life and the vision blockers you have overcome. I want to hear about the challenges you face and to celebrate your accomplishments with you.

Send an email with your thoughts, a text with your comments, or give me a phone call. I would like to hear from you.

Email: Eric@EricScroggins.com

Cellphone: 206-999-9748

Finally, I want to wish you the very best and all the success, love, and prosperity in life as you overcome all of your vision blockers.

Your Friend,

Dr. Eric Scroggins

About the Author

Dr. Eric Scroggins is an author, professional keynote speaker, executive leadership coach, banker, and pastor. He has a passion for seeing people reach their greatest potentials in everything they do. For the past twenty years, Eric has worked in various capacities from top performing "outside the box thinking" banker to senior pastor for two growing churches. He has taught on the topics of leadership, sales, personal development, vision, change, and financial management for personal, business, and organizational success.

Education, experience, and passion are enhanced when combined with real-life experience. Eric brings these elements together to deliver a dynamic and unique service to individuals, businesses, and organizations. Holding degrees in several fields, including a Bachelor of Science in business management, an MBA, and a Doctorate in Pastoral Psychology, he is well poised to deliver effective strategies and inspiration to those ready to change their lives.

Eric has not led a life free of personal struggle, but through those struggles, he has developed what is known now as "cultivated insight." Cultivated insight comes from a combination of solid education and professional experience along with having learned life's lessons as they come. He uses this cultivated insight to help the people who have reached out to him in an effort to change their lives.

Eric is also the founder of M6 Global Resources, a non-profit resource generator that assists other non-profit organizations in meeting their objectives. M6 Global Resources raises capital to invest in humanitarian relief efforts in the United States and abroad. Whether feeding hungry elementary school students, sending aid to disaster-struck villages, or rebuilding homes in war-torn Iraq, M6 Global Resources reaches out to ease the pain and suffering faced by humans every day. To assist M6 Global Resources in bringing hope to the hopeless, please consider making a tax deductible donation at www.M6GlobalResources.com

ABOUT DR. ERIC SCROGGINS

Executive Leadership Coaching

Dr. Eric Scroggins successfully coaches individuals, entrepreneurs, business leaders, pastors, and leaders for nonprofit organizations on breaking through barriers and winning at every level. Over the past twenty years, Dr. Scroggins has become recognized as one of the most sought-after keynote and conference speakers around. His direct and engaging approach of self-discovery and no more excuses helps eliminate what's standing in your way so you can develop the confidence needed to overcome all obstacles.

Eric's system includes one-on-one coaching sessions coupled with weekly conference calls and personal mentoring that will help you reach farther, gain more productivity, and win more often. Eric will help you build a strategy to achieve your sales goals faster, and help you lead your company to higher success by building in a leadership framework that encourages, inspires, and produces results. Your non-profit can raise the money you need to perform your mission, learn how to recruit the kinds of volunteers who make a difference, and reach further into the lives of the people you serve.

You can reach higher and accomplish more! Release your vision today!

For a thirty-minute complimentary consultation, contact:
www.EricScroggins.com

BOOK DR. ERIC SCROGGINS TO SPEAK AT YOUR NEXT EVENT

When it comes to choosing a professional speaker for your next event, you'll find no one more respected with more insight, no one who will leave your audience or colleagues with such a sense of enthusiasm, passion for life, and a "can do" attitude as Dr. Eric Scroggins. Eric is one of the most gifted communicators of our generation, and since 1991, he has been delivering dynamic messages of hope and inspiration to audiences around the world.

Whether your audience is 10 or 10,000, in North America or abroad, Eric can deliver a tailor-made message of inspiration that will leave your audience mesmerized and ready for more. Eric's speaking philosophy is to ensure that he connects with the audience members and understands their greatest desires. He knows that audiences want to hear real-life stories about real people that can help them relate the message to achieving their own destinies. It isn't uncommon to find Dr. Scroggins engaging with the audience prior to and after the presentation, making a human connection and inspiring participants to reach beyond their perceived limitations.

As a result, Eric's speaking style incorporates humor, stories, information, and above all, inspiration that gives the audience a sense of passion to achieve extraordinary results. If you are looking for a speaker who will leave a lasting impression and cause your audience to take action, then book Dr. Eric Scroggins today.

To see a highlight video of Eric and learn whether he is available for your next meeting, visit his website below and then contact him to schedule a complimentary pre-speech interview:

www.EricScroggins.com
Eric@EricScroggins.com
206-999-9748